SKYE PIONEERS AND "THE ISLAND"

Skye Pioneers

and

"The Island"

MALCOLM A. MACQUEEN

Selkirk
STORIES

ISBN 978-1-926494-27-2

Originally published in 1929.

Skye Pioneers and "The Island" is in the public domain.

Introduction Copyright © John Westlie 2018

Map of Uigg Lots redrawn from original by

A. Michael Shumate

To the sister, who from the day when, hand in hand, she guided the steps of a timid brother for the first time to school, has been his wise and constant friend.

"Ye dreams of my boyhood, how
much I regret you,
Unfaded your memory dwells in my breast;
Though sad and deserted, I ne'er can
forget you:
Your pleasure may still be in fancy possest."

TABLE OF CONTENTS

viii

Introduction

Malcolm Macqueen and the Writing of *Skye* *Pioneers*

Prince Edward Island in the 1880s saw a renewed interest in the past. Existing groups like the Caledonia Club saw revivals, while new groups such as the Historical Society of PEI were born. This renewed interest may have arisen from the demographic situation of Prince Edward Island following Confederation in 1873. While the population of Canada as a whole rose by a third in the first decade of the twentieth century, the population of Prince Edward Island was in steady decline. There was a net loss of almost 10% in the same decade, and an even greater reduction in the Scottish population. This was due to out-migration, with most emigrants going to the United States (mostly Boston, but also the western frontier, where there were opportunities for homesteaders). Those remaining on the Island may well have felt a sense of urgency to chronicle the history of a disappearing community. Malcolm Macqueen was one of the first to do so.

Skye Pioneers and 'The Island' (1929) by Malcom Macqueen (1878-1960) is one of the first works of genealogy and family history published in

Canada. A search for publications between 1880 and 1930 with the subject keyword "genealogy" in the *Voilà* database of Library and Archives Canada produces numerous results, but only 21 of these were published in the Maritime provinces or concern Maritime families, some in more than one edition. None concern immigrants from Skye. *Skye Pioneers and 'The Island'* may well be the first published book devoted to the settlers who came from Scotland, and specifically the Isle of Skye, to Prince Edward Island. This makes it a unique part of Canadian heritage.

Malcolm Macqueen was born on December 8, 1878, on the Uigg Road in Orwell, the son of John Angus Macqueen (1836-1918) and Isabella Nicholson (1845-1926), one of nine children. (Interested readers will find the entire Macqueen family tree on the Island Register website, www.islandregister.com). Macqueen proudly traced his own family back to the "Lords of the Isles" in Part Three of *Skye Pioneers*, beginning in the 12th Century with The Great Somerland, *Rex Insularum* ("king of the isles") and ending modestly with his own name and the name of his brother as the last of the line. He was particularly proud to be descended from Flora MacDonald, the Jacobite heroine who helped the Pretender, Bonnie Prince Charlie, escape to Skye after his defeat at the Battle of Culloden (1745).

Malcolm Macqueen is a graduate of the Uigg School, renowned for the accomplishments of its graduates. Macqueen makes much of the Uigg School in *Skye Pioneers*, both in Part One of the book, where he devotes a section to Uigg Grammar School, and in Part Two, where he enumerates the graduates (including himself) and their achievements. People today often attribute the accomplishments of graduates of the Uigg School, particularly considering to its low enrolment — there were never more than forty families in the district — to the high level of teaching and advanced curriculum, going beyond the three R's. Macqueen describes the curriculum as including Latin, algebra, French, and geometry. But the same level of teaching was not offered to all. Sir Alexander Macphail, in an article in the Charlottetown *Patriot*, explains: "A boy must prove that he was one of the few capable of learning ... In any year not more than three boys were considered qualified to profit from books ... These three were set apart, and upon them the master lavished all his care. He offered two forms of education, his undivided attention and his undivided neglect ... " (December 28, 1937). Macqueen must have been one of those benefiting from the master's undivided attention.

Upon leaving the Uigg School, Macqueen entered Prince of Wales College. This too was a rare privilege. Macqueen explains that "[e]very family strives to give higher education to at least one son. The parents and other children undergo all the privations necessary to attain this desired end." In the case of the Macqueen family, Malcolm appears have been the chosen one. His older brother James was a miner in the western United States, his brother Peter a farmer on Prince Edward Island, and his brother George went to Manitoba like Malcolm, but died as a young man.

Macqueen remained at Prince of Wales long enough to complete the courses enabling him to sit for the examinations for a teacher's certificate. The 1899 *Annual Report of the Public Schools* lists him as Principal of Uigg School. The school under Macqueen's leadership is praised in Appendix D of the report, Remarks on Schools Deserving Special Mention: "This School is maintaining its reputation for good work. Both teachers are careful and efficient."

Macqueen did like other teachers in the Uigg School he describes in *Skye Pioneers*: "They generally taught for two or three years and then pursued a course of higher study in universities in the other provinces ..." Macqueen graduated from Queen's University in Kingston, Ontario, in 1903 with a Bachelor of Arts degree. The curriculum for the Bachelor of Arts, as indicated by the examinations for the degree listed in the 1902-1903

Calendar of Queen's College and University, suggests a general course of study without what we
would today call a major. Although he was to
become a barrister, he did not formally study law.
At that time no instruction in law was offered at
Queen's University, although the degree of LL.D.
was awarded upon successfully writing an examination over a list of required legal texts. Those
permitted to sit for the examination were already
barristers-at-law or students-at-law as appointed
by the Law Society of Upper Canada.

In 1904, Macqueen went west to Winnipeg,
where he would make his home for the rest of his
life. He studied law as an apprentice in the firm
of Munro and West. Apprenticeship was the only
way to acquire a legal education in Manitoba at
this time. In 1908, Macqueen was a partner in the
firm. By 1913, the focus of Macqueen's business
had changed to real estate law. His law practice
shared an office suite with two other businesses:
W. R. Hamilton and Company, real estate; and
Major Schurman, a fellow Islander from the prominent Schurman family of Summerside. It appears
that Major Schurman acquired and developed
properties, while W. R. Hamilton promoted and
sold them. Macqueen and his fellow barristers
provided the needed legal services.

Real estate would have been a highly lucrative
business, although speculative, because Winnipeg

in the early years of the twentieth century was booming. By 1912, Winnipeg was the third largest city in Canada, dominating the industry and agriculture of western Canada. The population was young (the majority being under 40 years of age) and culturally diverse.

On November 20, 1912, Macqueen married Harriet Murgatroyd ("Maud") Riley, daughter of Robert T. Riley, one of the most prominent and influential men in Winnipeg. We can surmise that a man of Riley's power and prominence would not have given the hand of his second daughter to a man who was not himself a promising businessman. The Macqueens appear to have prospered. In 1922, there was a three-month holiday in Scotland and another extended trip to Scotland in 1929. A letter from Malcolm Macqueen dated January 27, 1927, includes this P.S.: "I am at present at suite 10, the Beverly, 1925 Nelson St., Vancouver, BC. Spending the winter away from the awful prairie cold." Newspaper social columns tell of the departure of Mrs. Macqueen and her father for Honolulu in 1928, and in 1932 she is reported to be returning from a stay in Victoria, B.C.

The couple had the means to be generous. In 1912, Malcolm Macqueen established the Macqueen Prizes at Prince of Wales College: $50, $30 and $20 respectively, awarded to the students writing the three best matriculation examinations in English. These were substantial amounts of money at the time. An article in the October 30, 1914, issue of the Charlottetown *Guardian* tells of Macqueen's donation of $20 per month to the Patriotic Fund, as well as his waiver of the rent on houses he owned whose tenants were at the front. The Macqueens' generosity extended beyond the war years into the Great Depression. The *Winnipeg Free Press* of November 4, 1932, lists Mr. and Mrs. Macqueen as having each donated $50 to the annual Community Chest drive.

Another indication of the Macqueens' affluence are their homes, which after 1927 were in the exclusive Armstrong's Point neighbourhood of Winnipeg. In 1927, after the death of his second wife, R. T. Riley invited Macqueen and his wife (who had no children) to live with him in his house at 186 Westgate, a stately Tudor mansion. The house, which still stands today, was recently listed for sale for just under $1 million, which suggests its size and elegance. After the death of Mr. Riley, Macqueen built a new home at 66 Westgate, in the same exclusive neighbourhood.

The obituaries of Malcolm Macqueen, published not only in Prince Edward Island and Manitoba newspapers but also in Ottawa, Toronto and other cities, state that he retired in 1918 to devote the rest of his life to research and writing on the subject of his native province. If this is true,

Macqueen would have been only forty years old. He would have been in law practice for only ten years and in the real estate business for about five years, judging by the listings in city directories. He may have earned enough by this time to live off the return on his investments. Macqueen gives this appraisal of Scottish thrift in Part One of *Skye Pioneers*: "The man who practises self denial and sets apart a portion of his earnings *to accumulate and work for him* ... attains wealth." But the words in italics seem more apt to 20th-century investment practices than to Skye pioneers and may well reveal the source of Macqueen's income.

Writing *Skye Pioneers* would have required time and travel. Since there is no record of any previously published written history of the Belfast community, we must assume that Macqueen gathered the information himself on one or more trips as well as through correspondence. The social columns of Island newspapers frequently include announcements of visits, such as the following: "Mr. Malcolm McQueen, Barrister, Winnipeg, is spending a short vacation with his parents, John M. and Mrs. McQueen, Orwell" (Charlottetown *Guardian*, October 9, 1915). But such announcements are rare, and we must rely on *Skye Pioneers* itself for clues into how Macqueen wrote it.

The book has three parts: the first part is a narrative that draws heavily on interviews with elderly Islanders, those who still had memories of the first settlers; the second part consists of documents, for most of which Macqueen gives a source; and the third part is genealogical tables ("Belfast Families"). While Macqueen may well have been researching the background to the book for years, there are hints within the text that suggest it was written shortly before publication. The informants Macqueen names in Part One are often said to have "recently" spoken or written about their memories. There are also dates woven throughout the book. Macqueen writes of a letter dated May 21, 1927, concerning renovations to St. John's Church, while we read that "on October 21, 1928, there was one headstone only standing erect" in the French cemetery in Belfast. In Part Two, the list of teachers in the Uigg and Orwell schools extends to 1929, the year *Skye Pioneers* was published. Some of the genealogies in Part Three bring the family tree to the late 1920s. Most importantly, following the account, in Part Two, of the celebrations of the Uigg centennial on August 17, 1929, Macqueen reflects on his own visit to Uig, Skye, "a few weeks before." Although we do not know the date of publication of *Skye Pioneers*, reviews of the book appear in Winnipeg and Prince Edward Island newspapers in late December 1929. All this suggests that the final version of the book was written in the autumn of

1929, after the Uigg centennial, and in time for a late fall publication.

Malcolm Macqueen died in Winnipeg General Hospital on April 21, 1960, after what newspapers call a long illness. He was survived by his wife. His will, surprisingly enough, directs "that no religious service of any kind be held before, at or after cremation." However, a service was held at a funeral home with the Rev. Rex R. Dolan presiding. His ashes were interred in the Old Kildonan Cemetery in Winnipeg.

Skye Pioneers appears to have three main goals. Part One seeks to give a voice to the past. Macqueen allows his informants to speak, quoting them at length whenever possible, and thereby preserving the voice of those who still remember the pioneering days on Prince Edward Island.

Part Three strives to connect past and present. The genealogies of the "Belfast Families" that Macqueen includes in his work connect the original settlers to those alive in 1929.

Part Two connects the past of Uigg, and by extension all the Skye pioneers, with the present. We read side by side tabulations of the original and 1929 tenants of the farms, as well as a list of the teachers of the Uigg and Orwell Schools from the earliest day to the present. We read of the memories evoked at the Uigg Centennial (1929) as well as the author's account of "Uigg of Today."

But perhaps most importantly, we read of the successful careers of the sons and daughters of Uigg who, like Macqueen, have left the province of their birth behind. This is the reason for the list of the achievements of graduates of the Uigg School as well as for the list of "distinguished sons and daughers of Belfast" who attended the Belfast Church (Saint John's Presbyterian Church). The greatest contribution of the Skye pioneers is to Canada and the world.

This is what is most apparent in the historical narrative that opens Part One of *Skye Pioneers*. Despite the tone of nostalgia and regret set by the epigraph to the book ("Ye dreams of my boyhood, how much I regret you ... Though sad and deserted, I ne'er can forget you ..."), this is a book about success. Macqueen's view of North America before and after European settlement would today would be considered at best as colonialist and condescending. European settlers have transformed a continent, turning "a wild waste" into "the happy home of many millions." In Macqueen's view, this is due in large part to the civilizing influence of the Highland Scots.

The thesis of *Skye Pioneers* is that the "success of major public enterprises in Canada" and especially in "the opening up and development of Canada, and of Western Canada in particular" is due to the Highland character. Macqueen distinguishes between culture (in which he deems the English and Irish more advanced) and character, where Scots have the upper hand. Unlike the Scot, the cultured English settler has "an eye trained to the beauty of the landscape." But the Scot, and especially the Highlander, has a character that lends itself to conquering a new world. The Scot, in Macqueen's view, is changeable and given to mood swings, like Macqueen's grandfather who can "pass from brooding melancholy to Highland gaiety with electric speed." Macqueen writes of a "sensitive and superstitious nature, tinged with brooding melancholy ... a restless spirit ... ardent sentiment and ready intuition." Macqueen seems to be implying that the restless Highland character leads to migration, first from the Old World to the New, then from east to west. This has benefited the new nation of Canada.

But it is not the Highland character alone that Macqueen praises, it is the specific traits of character embodied by Presbyterian settlers. Macqueen's account is concerned only with two groups of immigrants: the Selkirk Settlers of 1803 and the immigrants of 1829 who settled Uigg. Concerning the former, Macqueen emphasizes that it is "a fact of high significance" that the majority of the 1803 pioneers were from Skye. This is an indirect way of ignoring the Roman Catholic minority from Uist who also arrived in 1803 aboard the *Oughton*, one of the three ships brought by the Earl of Selkirk to Prince Edward Island. Macqueen is only concerned with Skye pioneers: the Presbyterians aboard the *Polly* and *Dykes*, the other two of Selkirk's ships, and the emigrants who arrived on the *Mary Kennedy* in 1829 and went on to found Uigg. They embody the true Highland character that Macqueen claims to have observed on his own visit to Skye in 1929:

> Character now as then is prized as in few other lands. It is only when one visits that misty island that a true measure can be taken of the extraordinary contribution Skye has made to Canada and other lands. Although so small an area, for generations it poured out in a steady stream its sons and daughters for the enrichment of those lands so fortunate to receive them as settlers. In their adopted homes Skye men and women have stamped the imprint of integrity and fidelity upon the life of the community and have earned ... an enviable reputation for honesty and obedience to law ...

The components of the Skye character are summed up in Macqueen's description of the Skye settlers of 1803. They had "unconquerable will and indomitable spirit. They were inured to hardship and unspoiled by luxury." They were successful in "tam[ing] the arrogance of nature" because of their "toil and self-denial." They are known for "independence, fearlessness, and self-reliance" as well as for "sobriety, industry and integrity." These traits of character, in Macqueen's view, are foundational to the institutions that make Canada great. He singles out the Hudson Bay Company, The Bank of Montreal, and the Canadian Pacific Railway as nation-building enterprises that owe their success to Scottish integrity.

Skye Pioneers is a pioneering work by a man whose life, like that of other graduates of the Uigg School or other "sons and daughters of Belfast," exemplifies the success that can follow from the self-denial and self-sacrifice of pioneers. He is the son who succeeded, who made good on his family's investment in his education. Although he continued to live a comfortable life in Winnipeg, he abandoned his career as quickly as it was financially feasible to devote himself to ensuring that the history of the Belfast community and the memory of the Skye character would never be forgotten. *Skye Pioneers and 'The Island'* has become the first stop for anyone investigating the history of Scottish settlement in North America. It is frequently cited as the source of information in later, better known, publications. As such, the book is itself a pioneer.

FOREWORD

by

James T. Mitchell, F.S.A. (Scot.), Editor,
Western Home Monthly

I am honored in being invited by the publishers to write a word or two in the form of an introduction to this most interesting volume from the pen of my good friend Malcolm A. Macqueen.

The author is a successful lawyer and man of affairs, as well as a facile writer, but he is more than that—he is a Highlander, with that pride of race surging through his blood-stream that has for years stimulated his people to high ideals and noble action—and that in brief has brought to the Gael the respect of all other peoples. Though three generations have separated him from the land of his fathers, the Isle of Skye, his enthusiasm has not grown cold, but rather have his affections for all that the Highlander stands for as a citizen of the Empire and a factor in the world's civilization been intensified. He combines with a strong admiration for the early Scottish Canadian pioneers, a mystical and spiritual love for all that is beautiful in life—a truly Hebridean characteristic.

The book will be received with a real joy not alone by his many friends throughout Canada and by his ain folk in his beloved Island home, Prince Edward, but by all who admire the perseverance, endurance and nobility of character displayed by those who faced the struggles of an unexplored land.

The narrative goes back to 1803 when Lord Selkirk arrived with his first Canadian settlement of Highlanders. Graphically and tenderly he takes up the story from the moment of the landing and traces his people in genealogical succession as well as their influence throughout all parts of the continent of America.

For this masterly labor of love no amount of research seemed too great or too tedious for the author. Indeed he has placed all of us whose hearts still go out in warmth to the old home across the seas, under a very deep obligation. While all other peoples manifest a regard for the place of their birth and the ashes of their fathers, it seems to me that in the Hebridean this worthy sentiment finds its most beautiful expression. Time and distance in his case do not weaken it—neither do generations efface it.

It was because of his admiration for those who set the path and blazed the trail that we are privileged to read a book of this nature—and a more worthy subject he could not have chosen.

Fortunate indeed is Canada or any other land that has among its intellectual citizens men like the author, who from the pressing exactitudes of professional, commercial and social life, take time to preserve memories that will always be an uplifting and patriotic influence.

ROIMH-RÀDH
LE SEUMAIS T. MITCHELL, F.S.A. (SCOT.), FEAR DEASACHAIDH NA DACHAIDH SIAR MHIOSAIL, WINNIPEG

Tha mi dha mheas na fhir onoir cuiridh fha-otiun bho luchd cho-bhuaileadh na hobrach so, gu focal no dha a channtain mun leabhar, shon-ruichte bho phean mo dheagh charaid, Calum MacCuinn (Malcolm Macqueen).

Tha n'ughdair maille ri bhi na fhear lagha soirbheachail, mar an ceudna na sgriobhaiche fior dheas labhrach, a thuilleadh air a sin is fior ghaidheal e aig a m-bheil uail mhor na reis agus na ghineal fein, chionn troimh a chuislean tha ruith gu laidir, fuil fhior ghlan nan-gaidheal. Tha e na phearsa fhein na eisempleir, ann a bhi bros-nachadh a dhaoine gu oidhirp an uaslachd agus an gniomh. Tha air an aobhar sin mor speis air a nochdadh dha le muinntir eile.

Ged tha tri ginealachain air a sgaradh bho dhuthaich a shinnsir san Eilean Sgiathanach, gid-headh tha e eudmhor ann an doigh shonruichte mu chleachdaidhean agus caithe beath a luchd duthcha anns gach cearnaidh de n-saoghail anns na cheadaich an crannachair dhaibh a bhi, Thuil-leadh air a speis agus uaill ais na ceud eilthireach, bho Albann. Tha muirn nach gann aige do nithean diomhair, agus spioradail, agus do na nithean bha priseal ann an caithe beath na n'eileanach.

Tha sinn fior chinnteach gu m-bith an leabhar so no aobhar aoibhneas cha nann a mhain dha chairdean an duthaich a bhreth is arach ann an Eilean Phrionnsa Eideard ach mar an cendu leis na huile neach aig a m-bheil meas air seasmhachd uaisleachd agus cliu laidir na muinntir a chuir an aghaidh air an duthaich neo-rannsaichte so anns na lathean bho chian.

Tha n-sgeul dol air ais gus a bhliadhna 1803, nuair a thainig na ceud eilthireach bho ghaidheal-tachd na-Halba maille ri Tighearna Selkirk. Gu dealbhach blath chridheach tha e toirt air adhairt na sguel, bhon a chuir iad a cheud chas air tir san talamh fhuar so, tha e feorach a mach ginelach an deigh ginealach, agus a bhuaidh a bha aca air luchd aiteachaidh na tir so.

Cha do mheas n'ughdair nith air bith na dragh ann an co-cheangail ris an obair a ghabh e bhos laimh ann a bhi cuir an leabhair ri cheile. Chuir e bho mhor chomain na huile neach dha mithich an cridhe bhi dol a mach ann a m-blaths sa n-carantas, gu tir na n-gleann na m-beann Sna n-gaisgeach.

Tha e gu haraid fior mu na gaidheal agus luchd aiteachaidh nan eileanaim mar is faide sgarar iad o n-duthaich gu m-bheil an gaol do thir an breth san arach fas nis treise sna s-treise, agus do luaithre an athraichean tha aca speis agus murn nach much tiom.

Sann air son a mhor speis bha aige do na daoine coire a lasrach sa dhealraich le n-eisempleir an duthaich so a chuir e n-leabhair taithneach so ri cheile agus a chuire e mhuinntir a leughas e bho mhor chomain.

Tha n-duthaich so, na duthaich air bith eile, fortainaich ann a bhi cunntadh a measg a luchd comhnaidh daoine mar an ughdair, tha fios-rach tuigseal agus spioradail anns na huile seol, a ghabhas uine agus a nith saothair chum sgu m-bith na nithean a bha cliutach agus ion-mholta anna m-beatha an sinnsir, air a theasraig, agus air a shionadh sios gun smal agus gun truail do n-al a thig na n-deigh.

Part One: Founding of Belfast

Lord Selkirk, The French, The *Polly*, Land Tenure

When Jacques Cartier, on June 20, 1534, discovered L'Isle St. Jean, the present Prince Edward Island, he found the trees there "Marvellously beautiful and pleasant in odour—cedars, pines, yews, white elms, ash trees, willows and others unknown. Where the land was clear of trees it was good, and abounded in red and white gooseberries, peas, strawberries, raspberries, and wild corn, like rye, having almost the appearance of cultivation. The climate was most pleasant and warm. There were doves and pigeons and many other birds."

Since then North America has been settled almost entirely by peaceful pioneer groups and individuals, mainly seeking greater freedom, either civil or religious, or wider opportunities for economic advancement. They and their descendants have, in three centuries, transformed a continent. They found a wild waste of dismal swamp and gloomy forest, abode of stealthy savage and majestic deer; treeless plain, alternately scorched by summer's blistering sun and chilled by winter's bitter blast; dark forbidding

mountain, temple of mystery. Where once the buf-
falo roamed in thundering millions the settler now
garners crops of golden corn. The iron rail and
metalled road displace the labored oar. Nature
has been subdued and broken by the will of man,
and today these wastes of yesterday provide the
happy home of many millions. The cost in human
toil and anguish of this, an accomplishment so
stupendous, can be estimated only by such as
reckon the vast number of those that shared the
toil and now lie sleeping in Earth's bosom.

A settlement of Highland Scots is believed to
have been made in North Carolina as early as
1739. Following the collapse of the rebellion in
1745, and the breaking down of the clan system,
a great wave of emigration from the Highlands of
Scotland set in. Fifty-four vessels full of emigrants
from the Western Isles and the Highlands sailed
for North Carolina between April and July, 1770.
In 1772 the great Macdonald emigration began
and lasted until the outbreak of the Revolutionary
War in 1776. Boswell in his "Journal of a Tour of
the Western Islands" made with Johnson in 1773,
refers to the eager enthusiasm of the people to
emigrate to the American Colonies. Up to this
time no emigrant from Skye had ever gone elsewhere than to North Carolina. Many people in
the Belfast district in Prince Edward Island, are
kinsmen of the Scots in that State.

In 1771 James Macdonald, merchant, Portree (Skeabost), and Norman Macdonald of Slate (Scalpa), for themselves and on behalf of Hugh Macdonald, of Armadale, Edmund Macqueen, John Betton, Alexander Macqueen of Slate, Rev. William Macqueen of Snizort, and Alexander Macdonald of Cuidrach, in Skye, petitioned the King's Majesty in Council for a grant of 40,000 acres of land in North Carolina, upon the usual terms and conditions of such grants. The petition was dismissed 19th June, 1772, by the Privy Council Committee on Plantation affairs on the ground that it was not desirable that so many people should leave the country.

The Revolutionary War put a temporary stop to the exodus to North Carolina. The Colony, however, was established firmly, and friends in the homeland soon began to join their kinsmen beyond the seas, regardless of the political separation from the Motherland.

The social unrest at the time of the American and the French Revolutions and the economic depression during and after the Napoleonic Wars, added further incentive to the already all-too-eager desire to emigrate, and by 1805 large numbers were departing to join their relatives and friends in the Carolinas.

During the period of this great emigration the Army claimed many recruits, and Skye men played a great part in deciding England's destiny on the field of battle. From about 1797 to 1837 it is computed that ten thousand private soldiers, six hundred commissioned officers under the rank of Colonel, forty-five Lieutenant-Colonels, twenty-one Lieutenant-Generals and Major-Generals, and one hundred and twenty pipers from the Isle of Skye were in the British Army. Skye, during the same period, gave four Governors of British Colonies, one Governor-General of India, and one Adjutant-General to the British Army. In the Battle of Waterloo it is computed sixteen hundred Skyemen fought in the British ranks.

In 1771 Thomas Douglas, youngest of the seven sons of the 4th Earl of Selkirk, was born. By 1799 his father and all his brothers were dead and he had succeeded to the title. He was destined for the law, and in Edinburgh was an associate of Jeffrey, Fergusson, Scott, and others of the leading spirits in that shining age. He was deeply interested in the problems of his time, and longed to ameliorate the hard lot of his fellow countrymen. He spent ten years abroad in travel and study, and in 1802, on his return home, proposed a national scheme designed to remedy the social unrest. The next eight years, from 1802 to 1811, were spent by him in an effort to divert the tide of emigration from the Carolinas to Eastern Canada. Thereafter his life was occupied in his endeavors to found the Selkirk

Colony on the banks of the Red River. He wished his fellow countrymen to establish themselves in circumstances providing full scope for their industry, and under the British flag. He first directed his efforts to Prince Edward Island. Three ships were chartered and about eight hundred passengers embarked to found a new home on his estate on this island. The *Polly* had the greatest number of passengers, most of whom were from Skye. On her was Dr. Angus MacAuley, agent for Selkirk. She arrived in Orwell Bay, Prince Edward Island, on Sunday, August 7, 1803, and disembarked her passengers near the present Halliday's Wharf. The *Dykes* arrived on August 9, and the *Oughton* with the Uist men on August 27. At this time the total population of the island was but little over five thousand. Selkirk, who was a passenger on the *Dykes*, had planned to arrive before the others so that preparations might be made for their reception, but before he appeared on the scene the *Polly* had disembarked her complement. "I arrived," he writes, "late in the evening, and it had then a very striking appearance. Each family had kindled a large fire near their wigwams, and round these were assembled groups of figures, whose peculiar national dress added to the singularity of the surrounding scene. Confused heaps of baggage were everywhere piled together beside their wild habitations, and by the number of fires the whole woods were illuminated. At the end of this line of encampment I pitched my own tent, and was surrounded in the morning by a numerous assemblage of people whose behaviour indicated that they looked to nothing less than a restoration of the happy days of Clanship." To obviate the terrors which the woods were calculated to inspire, the settlement was not dispersed, as those of the Americans usually are, over a large tract of country, but concentrated within a moderate space. The lots were laid out in such a manner that there were generally four or five families, and sometimes more, who built their houses in a little knot together; the distance between the adjacent hamlets seldom exceeding a mile.

Each of them was inhabited by persons nearly related, who sometimes carried on their work in common, or at least were always at hand to come to each other's assistance.

"The settlers had every inducement to vigorous exertion from the nature of their tenures. They were allowed to purchase in fee simple, and to a certain extent on credit; from fifty to one hundred and fifty acres were allotted to each family at a very moderate price, but none was given gratuitously. To accommodate those who had no superfluity of capital they were not required to pay the price in full till the third or fourth year of their possession.

"I left the Island in September, 1803, and after an extensive tour on the continent, returned in the end of the same month the following year. It was with the utmost satisfaction I then found that my plans had been followed up with attention and judgment.

"I found the settlers engaged in securing the harvest which their industry had produced. They had a small proportion of grain, of various kinds, but potatoes were the principal crop. These were of excellent quality, and would have been alone sufficient for the entire support of the settlement."

That his schemes of settlement were to be a panacea for all the ills disturbing the State was not the expectation of the generous-minded Selkirk. "I will not assert," he says, "that the people I took there have totally escaped all difficulties and discouragements, but the arrangements for their accommodation have had so much success that few people perhaps in their situation have suffered less, or have seen their difficulties so soon at an end."

Although the circumstances under which Lord Selkirk settled the Red River district in Rupert's Land, and the Belfast district in Prince Edward Island had much similarity, the peculiar isolation under which the Red River settlers lived for upwards of sixty or seventy years led to an intense loyalty to the founder of the colony, and to the colony itself as a social and political institution. A thousand miles of wilderness, of lakes, forests, and rivers, lay to the east; the great plains to the south and west, occupied by warring tribes of hostile Indians. There was left one road only of ingress to and egress from the colony. This meant a trying journey by boat and canoe from the settlement through Lake Winnipeg, and the Hayes or the Nelson River to Hudson's Bay. From there, an ocean voyage in stormy ice-beset northern latitudes to England. All but the bravest shrank from such a journey. From 1812 until 1870 the Selkirk colonists on the banks of the Red River lived largely unto themselves, and to this day they are as loyal to the Selkirk settlement and to the Selkirk tradition as is any Highlander to his clan chief.

Not so the Selkirk colony on Prince Edward Island. Three years before they arrived the total population of the Island was about five thousand; that of Charlottetown about two hundred and fifty to three hundred. Only a few miles distant from them to the north, a settlement of Loyalists from the American colonies had been founded along Vernon river in 1792. They preferred to endure the hardships incident to founding a new home in the virgin forest under the flag they loved, than live under a government they regarded as alien to the political principles they espoused. The Selkirk colonists, after a generation, ceased to look upon themselves as a separate institution, and merged their lives in the larger life of the little province in which they lived. Today the Selkirk tradition is largely forgotten except by those who pursue it historically for intellectual diversion.

In culture and civilization the Scots and Irish were much behind the English. Even to this day they have not reached the same degree of culture as their more wealthy neighbors. Owing to the poverty of his country the Highlander is unable to acquire many of the comforts essential to cultural development. From a state almost bordering on naked barbarism, in a comparatively short time, they had settled down to an ordered social life. Even before the great migration began after "the Forty-five," raids on neighboring clans to avenge either some real or fancied personal or clan injury, or to fill the empty larder, had become of but infrequent occurrence.

Steady unremitting toil is alien to the Highland nature. The drudgery of the farm makes less appeal to him than does work in the mysterious forest, on the changing ocean, or in any other calling responsive to a spirit emotional and imaginative. His highly sensitive and superstitious nature, tinged with brooding melancholy, requires change and diversity. As a consequence we find him at his best in a vocation which appeals to his restless spirit, and makes frequent calls upon his ardent sentiment and ready intuition. Seafaring, because the Viking ancestral spirit is in his blood, and the learned professions, because of the diversity of work, suit him best. In these he has been a notable success, and has left the imprint of sturdy Scottish character and Scottish integrity upon society in every part of the world in which his lot has been cast, and where duty has called him.

How much these qualities in the Scot have had to do with the success of the major public enterprises in Canada is a matter of interesting speculation. The Scot himself may claim the chief honor. Many others will willingly grant him a very large share of the credit where success has been achieved. Certainly in the opening up and development of Canada, and of Western Canada in particular, the Scot has played a dominant part.

In the City of London, under the presidency of that swashbuckling ruffian, Rupert of the Rhine, there was incorporated on the 2nd of May, 1670, "the Governor and Company of Adventurers of England trading into Hudson's Bay." Being primarily fur traders this Company strove to retain for themselves, as was their legal right, exclusive control of the trade of the vast territories granted to them. They always looked askance at settlement, and regarded with jealous eye the advent of anyone from outside their employ. It is true that their policy retarded the settlement and development of the country for generations, and that of late years it has been the practice, though an unworthy one, to disregard their monumental services to Canada, and, ignoring history, to condemn the Company, as if in their long and enviable record there was nothing to commend. In the annals of trade and commerce the name "Hudson's Bay Company" will ever stand apart, conspicuous alike in romance of origin and honorable achievement. A beacon of honesty for more than a quarter of a thousand years, it has stood between the rapacity of the white man and the credulity of the simple minded native, to whom it has ever been the visible token and symbol of justice, of humanity, and of fair dealing. The "true and absolute Lords and Proprietors," it set and adhered to a fixed standard of barter between itself and those over whose lives it was Destiny personified. By frugal distribution it raised the supply of food and clothing, the absolute necessities of human life, from precarious uncertainty to definite certainty, and thereby saved the simple minded native from the misery and degradation of alternate feast and famine.

To the poor Indian, whose standard of living has been fixed by an unchanging system of just and honest exchange for hundreds of years, the advantage has been incalculable. The assurance of certain and ample reward for service, the unvarying justice, the fixity of value in the system of barter, raised him from a creature of momentary splendor and as swift poverty, to definite self respectability and dignity. Nor has the world ever seen a more fitting and constant appreciation and return for paternal care and self assumed responsibility on the part of the Company than it has received from its willing wards during the full course of its beneficent history. True to its watchword — *pro pelle cutem* — the Company soon became, as indeed it was and continued to be in the person of its agents, the physical symbol of justice, order and authority. In place of the frequent outbreaks of cruel lawlessness and open warfare between the red and the white man, so common in regions less fortunately governed, and not so far distant, there is here presented the spectacle of an institution, with posts scattered over a territory ranging from two thousand to three thousand miles square, manned by a few whites, living with the natives not only in peaceful harmony and perfect safety, but on terms of willingly admitted superiority and authority. Nor in the long history of the Company has this moral authority ever been challenged. Rarely, if ever, has the fair name "Hudson's Bay Company" been besmirched by cruelty, injustice or fraudulent practice. Never has the sovereign power of which it was the visible agent, been demeaned in the eye of the credulous native by any lawless act of theirs. Not by statutory authority, but rather by humane treatment and fair dealing, did it become the living symbol of British authority, and of British justice, and as such was it recognized by them. In estimating the honorable part which this great Company has played in preserving huge territories to the nation, and attempting to hold other valuable areas which were lost through causes not within its control, tribute in unstinted measure must be paid to that noble band of Scots who, since they first entered the Company's employ to the present day, have been recruited and sent overseas to man those remote outposts of Empire in the hidden wastes of a vast continent, unseen and unheard except by those whose destiny they held in sacred trust. Whatever the future may hold in store for fair Scotia, those of her blood may look back with unfeigned pride upon the record of her sons' great share in guiding the Company's affairs with success so signal, and in moulding the early life of a new nation on the sure footing of justice, law and order.

This humane and historic Company, throughout its whole career, adapted itself to changing circumstances and surroundings. It assumes new shape and form to meet the varied circumstances of the passing hour, and thus lives on, symbol of an honored past and inspiration to a greater future.

Intimately connected with this Company is that other great institution carried on with unvarying success through a period of over a century by men largely of Scottish blood and tradition—The Bank of Montreal.

It commands a position of the highest honor not only in Canada, but in the world. The cardinal policy of this bank through the whole course of its long existence has been never to compromise fundamentals for any questionable gain, however great. On this firm foundation the sagacity of its directors and managers has built up an institution which today is an honor to the foresight of its counsels, to the character of the people, and to the Government of Canada.

The same Scottish tradition inspired the founding and guided the early operation of that other great institution, the Canadian Pacific Railway Company. The fact that men of Scottish race have fashioned these three world-encompassing institutions brings a glow of well merited pride to the cheek of everyone possessing Scottish blood.

Being an enlightened reformer Selkirk threw the greatest possible responsibility on the shoulders of the settler, and "the industry of the individual settler was allowed full scope to exert itself."

The Island had been divided into sixty-six Lots

or Townships. In 1767 it was granted to various persons, some of whom were officers in the Army and Navy, others were merchants and members of Parliament. These Lots, which were acquired by ballot, went in some cases to one person, in others to several. When one person was to get a whole Lot his name alone appeared on a slip of paper, otherwise several names appeared on the slip as sharers in one Lot. Lot 57 fell to Sam Smith and Captain James Smith, R.N., of the *Seahorse*. It later became part of the Selkirk Estate, and on the shore of this Lot the Scottish settlement was made in 1803. Lot 50, adjoining, fell by lot to Lieut.-Colonel H. Gladwin and Peter Innis. The various proprietors were required to settle the land, but few carried out the conditions of the grant. The quit rents to which these lands were subject were adjusted on the basis of 6s., 4s. and 2s. per hundred acres. For the first five years after the grant no quit rents were payable. For the next five years one-half the fixed rents were payable. After ten years the whole amount was payable. Even though these rents were later reduced, they were still an intolerable burden on the new settlers, and for generations there was a growing discontent with the leasehold tenure of land, culminating in an agitation of such intensity that it was not stilled until 1860, when the Government appointed a commission of enquiry. This led to the Government purchase of the land from the landlords, and the sale of it to the various purchasers. Leasehold tenure was changed to freehold, and with its assurance of permanency the owner had every incentive to improve his property. This he speedily did, with results so satisfactory that material prosperity and mental content advanced hand in hand. In 1860 the Selkirk Estates in Lots 53, 57, 58, 59, 60 and 62, containing 62,059 acres, were purchased by the Government for £6,386 17s. 8d. sterling, or £9,880 6s. 6d. currency.

The settlement, afterwards called Belfast, a corruption of the French "La Belle Face," was founded on the abandoned site of a French colony whose members were deported to France after the surrender of Louisburg in 1758. Their settlement extended along the coves and creeks from the mouth of Charlottetown harbor to the Pinette River. A French naval officer who visited the various French settlements on the Island in 1752 reported that the number of settlers in this area was not less than five hundred. Later the whole territory from Vernon River to Wood Islands extending inland a few miles was, and is now known generally as, the Belfast District.

The clearing had again grown up, but various evidences of the former occupation, the shallow well, the ditch, still existed. The old cemetery that knew the voice of the Curé, M. Gerard, with its pathetic reminders of the transitory career of man, was soon requisitioned by the newcomers to fill the purposes for which it was dedicated, and today former members of a district settled with similar hopes, but alien in race and religion, sleep in undisturbed repose within the sacred confines of the common hallowed spot.

The majority of the 1803 settlers were from Skye, a fact of high significance. In that inhospitable island, from the dawn of its recorded history, was bred a race of men and women of unconquerable will and indomitable spirit. They were inured to hardship and unspoiled by luxury. Living in a land distant and inaccessible, they there maintained in their isolation, to an unusual degree, racial purity and distinctive racial characteristics. These qualities were carried across the seas to America, and there they were further developed. In the environment peculiar to their island, Skyemen developed into a military aristocracy undaunted by hardship or danger. Having been tried in the fires of adversity for generations they were a band well chosen to tame the arrogance of nature in the forests of Belfast. But this was not accomplished without toil and self-denial unknown to those who attempt a similar work in an age ministered to by all the comforts provided by modern science. The isolation of their new home, and the persistent intermarriage between members of the same stock, have tended to maintain those characteristics peculiar to them, to a degree almost unknown in other parts of English speaking Canada.

Although the Belfast settlers were to a large extent isolated in their new homes, they never wholly forgot the land of their forefathers. In song and story, to this day, one finds constant evidence of the strong spiritual bond uniting the two islands, and the intense loyalty of the early settlers to the Skye tradition burns in the breast of the present generation with a flame as steady as it did in any that has gone before. All are haunted by the same dreams.

> "From the lone shieling of the misty island,
> Mountains divide us and the waste of seas;
> Yet still the blood is strong, the heart
>   is Highland,
> And we in dreams behold the Hebrides."

The recent call to battle met a ready response, and many of the youth of Belfast sleep in "Flanders Fields" beside their Skye kinsmen, fired by the same purpose, all "brave sons of Skye." Thus was verified almost two hundred years after, the character ascribed to these people by the great Pitt (afterwards Earl of Chatham), in addressing the House of Commons, when he said: "I have sought for merit wherever it could be found. It is my boast that I was the first Minister who looked for it, and found it in the mountains of the North. I called it forth, and drew into your service a hardy and intrepid race of men; men who, when left by your jealousy, became a prey to the artifices of your enemies, and had gone nigh to have overturned the State in the war before last. These men in the last war were brought to combat on your side; they served with fidelity, as they fought with valour in every quarter of the globe."

Perhaps no quality characterized the Scottish race more than their love of education. They realize, as few other peoples, that knowledge is the sesame that opens wide the magic door to a life of wider prospect with all the increased privileges and added sorrows that go with it. Every family strives to give higher education to at least one son. The parents and other children patiently undergo all the privations necessary to attain this desired end. The religious outlook of Scotland, of which their school system is an expression, has done more, perhaps, than any other agency to inculcate that proud spirit in the race which encourages the young to feel that there is no position in society to which the individual may not aspire. For this reason the Scot is distinguished for his independence, fearlessness, and self-reliance. As an organizer and administrator he is imaginative, far-seeing and resourceful. As an empire builder he is without a superior. In whatever part of the world one may go, wherever the English language is spoken, one finds in the forefront in every walk of life descendants of that sturdy stock of pioneers who owe their start in life to the sound example set before them in youth, of sobriety, industry and integrity.

It may be expected that the Selkirk settlers brought with them to their new home this ardent desire for the better and higher things of life. If they could not have such for themselves they were all the more anxious that their children should have what they themselves were denied. During the first few years in the colony facilities for formal education were of the most meagre kind. Soon, however, well trained Skye schoolmasters opened up, in private homes, their little academies of learning, and here the neighboring children gathered, eager for instruction. The name of the first teacher is not definitely known, but it is alleged by some that the first school in the settlement was conducted in a log cabin in the Pinette district by Donald Nicholson, a Skye man, who arrived on the *Polly* in 1803. Others maintain it was beside the French cemetery. It was not until 1821 that the Government prepared to open national schools.

In 1826 a general School Act was passed. It was re-enacted in 1830. Section four of said Act enacts that "any person who may be a candidate for the office of master or teacher in any grammar or district school within this Island shall, on one of the days of said meetings, or on such other days as any three of the said Board shall appoint, present himself for and shall submit to an examination of his qualifications in the following branches of education—that is to say, candidates for the office of master or teacher of any district school, in reading the English language, writing, practical arithmetic and the elements of English grammar; and for the office of master or teacher of a grammar school in the Latin and Greek classics usually taught in schools, the elements of English grammar, reading the English language, writing, arithmetic, practical mathematics and geography – And if the Board shall be satisfied with the candidate's proficiency, they shall give him a certificate of his having passed such examination which certificate shall express the nature of the school for which the candidate has passed examination."

Prior to 1826 there were no prescribed subjects of study, but Mr. John Anderson, at present Provincial Auditor of P.E.I., who was born in Orwell Cove, recalls hearing in fireside conversation when a young boy, that reading lessons were given from whatever books were available.

Needless to say the Bible and the Shorter Catechism were used most. The value to the pupil
of daily instruction in the Bible by a man who
prized it as a literary masterpiece no less than
as an infallible guide to conduct, was priceless.
The other subjects, Writing, Spelling, Grammar,
Geography, and Arithmetic were no doubt taught
without the aid of textbooks.

In 1823 Rev. John MacLennan became the
incumbent in Belfast. From the day when that
noble spirit arrived in the district until he departed
from it, his strength was given without stint to
aid and uplift those among whom he lived and
labored. He soon opened a school at Pinette, and
in addition to his many other arduous and trying
duties, he taught there for years. Strange as it may
seem, there were even then, in the humble homes
of Belfast, pupils who craved a knowledge of the
classics. Mr. MacLennan taught them Latin in
addition to the ordinary subjects. His work was
highly commended by John MacNeill, Inspector of Schools, in his report to the government,
in 1841.

In reporting to the government in 1838 Mr.
MacNeill uses a table which shows the limited
curriculum of that time. [Readers, Spelling Books,
First Books and Arithmetic are the only textbooks.]

Before two generations had passed the number
of professional men coming from this district

proved that the spirit of their forefathers had taken deep root in the soil of the new world. Many families contributed members, in some cases as many as seven, to the learned professions and to business life. No self-denial on the part of any member of the household was considered too great if thereby one of the family, who desired it, was enabled to pursue his studies at a seat of higher learning. Medicine and engineering were looked upon with great favor, and the career of any youth who entered one of these professions was watched with eager interest. The Church too was favored by many, and the early organization of a highly devotional congregation, presided over by ministers of wide knowledge and broad sympathy, did much to hold it in the esteem and affection of the people long after it had begun to lose its power in other parts. Few congregations of similar size have given as many sons to the active ministry of the Church. The highly imaginative Highlander, with his love of meditation, found in the pulpit a fitting medium to express without reserve, the intensity of the gloomy forebodings which ever characterized his theory of life and religion.

Owing to the prospect, not always remote, of political preferment incident to the legal profession, it was looked upon by many as a most desirable calling. Coupled with this was the more fixed home life of those following this vocation. Its vagaries and opportunities for disputation made it congenial to the peculiar mental constitution of the Highlander, with his alternate periods of brooding melancholy and infectious gaiety. They were farseeing enough to recognize the high value of a legal training as a matter of mental discipline, and the consequent benefits accruing to the student of law in any calling one might choose. They also realized the great truth expressed by Edmund Burke, "The law is a science which does more to quicken and invigorate the understanding than all the other kinds of learning put together." It is not therefore to be wondered at that, with such an outlook on life, this district gave a large number of men of high integrity and skill to the bench and bar.

But the great majority, as in other parts, were unable to attain a formal higher education. In the ranks of these, one finds men and women of the highest honor and fidelity, whose lives have been not only a credit to themselves and a source of pride to their families, but an honor to their native land.

IN THEIR NEW HOMES

As summer was almost over when the settlers landed they erected at once rude cabins to shelter them from the bitter cold of winter then approaching. These were built of logs squared and dovetailed at the ends. The spaces between were filled with moss or clay. The seams were covered with birch bark. Over all a ply of boards was nailed. The roof was covered with pine shingles. The nails used in this work were of iron, made by a blacksmith in the settlement. The windows in these little cabins were few and small as glass was dear. It took iron courage to face the first winter in this inhospitable climate, and until the harvest was garnered next autumn their minds were harassed often by the grim spectre of want hovering about their kitchen door.

Entering the humble cottage of the early settler one found an abode of Arcadian simplicity. If at meal time, there might be half a dozen healthy blue-eyed children, with their parents, seated on planks around the rough board table. The simple fare consisted of potatoes and pickled herring or dried salt cod. Oatmeal porridge was the staple breakfast dish. It was many years later before wheat flour was used daily. In the meantime, barley and buckwheat varied the oatmeal diet. Many meals were partaken without forks and knives, and those in use were made generally of horn. The teapot was always on the hearth. The Scots were inordinately fond of tea and drank copious quantities of that beverage. As soon as a caller entered the house the kindly housewife, with unbounded hospitality, proffered a cup.

Of adornments there were none. The walls and ceilings were of untouched native wood. Later it was customary to whitewash the whole interior with slaked lime. This sanitary practice continued until wallpaper was introduced.

The bedstead consisted of a rough hewn frame on which lay a huge home-made linen tick, filled with grass, and in later years the choicest oat chaff. This made a warm, clean and comfortable resting place. At least once a year, at threshing, it was emptied and refilled. As a supply of chaff for ticks was stored in the barns they could be changed whenever the housewife so desired.

As domestic geese were raised in large numbers, feather ticks became common and the guest chamber was generally equipped with one. The houses were cold. The open chimney, although healthful, allowed most of the heat to pass off without tempering the air in the chilly rooms. Beside the fireplace hung the boot-jack, fashioned from the crotch of birch or maple, while over it rested an old Queen Anne rifle. Newspapers were unknown. Other books were rare, but the Gaelic Bible was in every home. By the fitful glow of the pine knot on the fireplace, the father read the nightly lesson from its sacred pages. All were warmly clothed. The men wore natural grey homespun, the women drugget. Their shoes were made in neighboring homes from cowhide tanned in the settlement. Well rubbed with warm sheep's tallow, they were impervious to water.

The settlers started at once cutting down the forest. "How bow'd the woods beneath their sturdy stroke." They reserved all marketable timber to be floated to the nearest shipping point for export the following summer, or to be converted into ships.

The Scots and Irish lacked the Englishman's deep appreciation of the beauty of the forest. In their eagerness to clear the land they swept everything bare, in many cases leaving neither hedges nor even shelters about their homes. The English settler, with an eye trained to the beauty of landscape, frequently brought acorns and shrubbery with him, and today one finds well laid out grounds that testify to the forethought and taste of these farseeing English pioneers. The Goff homestead at Woodville, Cardigan, is an example. Only in the past generation have the Scots made consistent efforts to beautify their homesteads by planting trees, and laying out their grounds in an orderly manner.

Not being experienced woodsmen the task of clearing the forest was very laborious and dangerous, occasionally resulting in serious injury and even death. But with experience they gained

knowledge, and within a few years the young men
became skilled in all the arts of woodcraft. Lum-
bering was the chief industry for many years. The
choicest timber was used in shipbuilding. In every
harbor along the coast were built ships, which,
manned by daring seamen, brought fame to their
native isle in every leading seaport throughout
the world. As early as 1825 large numbers were
launched, and in that year forty vessels of 8,409
tons were built. The shipwrights' hours of labor
were long. Frequently several miles intervened
between the shipyard and the workman's home.
One lady recently told of her father, over seventy
years ago, walking daily, six miles to and from
his work at Davies' shipyard. His honesty, so
characteristic of the times, was such that on one
occasion, finding a few iron spikes in his pocket
when he got home, he insisted on bringing them
back next day, for, as he said, if he did not do so
they might be in his coffin.

Occasional trees, especially pine, were of imposing size. On each farm, for many years after the
forest was cleared, isolated stumps stood in the
cultivated fields, silent reminders of the venerable
monarchs that once looked down from imposing heights upon the meaner growth of maple,
spruce, birch, beech and fir around them. On one
of these farms, near a grateful spring, stood a
notable stump, six feet in diameter. This remnant

of a lordly pine withstood decay for over half a century. Finally, about 1900, it succumbed to the annual attacks of fire and axe.

Potato sets, with one eye, were planted in groups of three or four and lightly covered with the rich soil and ash from the recent fire. After the young plant showed above the ground it was "killed." As there were no pests (the Colorado beetle or "potato bug" attacked them first about 1895), and but few weeds, they were not touched again. They yielded about twenty-fold next fall. Wheat, oats and barley, which were sown among the stumps broadcast also gave bountiful yields.

Until the land was stumped all grain was cut with reaping hooks. When the clearing was large enough, the back-breaking cradle was used. This instrument consisted of an iron blade or scythe and cradle with four hardwood fingers, adjusted to the handle. The grain fell across the fingers. The cradler strove to lay the grain in an even swath on the highest stubble to lighten the work of the binder, who followed with a hand rake. While binding the sheaf the harvester rested the handle on his shoulder. In this spot the skin was soon calloused. It is reported of one Neil Campbell, of Peel County, Ontario, that he took a swath eleven feet wide and cut eleven acres in a day. Five acres was considered a good day's cradling in average grain not broken or tangled. Cutting started before the grain was ripe. Ripened straw became so brittle in the hot sun that sometimes it could not be used for bands. In such cases binding was done in the evening and morning, when the straw was softened by the dew.

Women cut much grain with the sickle, but rarely with the cradle. "Oft did the harvest to their sickle yield." They bound, after the cradle, though hampered by their long skirts and often barefoot. The torture caused by the sharp stubble and prickly thistles, was almost unbearable.

The reaper, drawn by two or three horses, displaced the cradle. A man, standing on the machine, raked the grain off the table. Later a revolving rake, set on a stand, swept the bundle from the table onto the ground. It could be adjusted so that, instead of every fourth rake carrying off the grain, the driver tripped it at will and made the sheaf the size desired.

Those who, under a burning sun, have bound grain infested with Canada thistle, will vividly recall the hardship of it. Even horny hands did not escape festering sores. Each year as the seeded acreage increased the burden grew heavier. Finally the self-binder brought relief from the cruel task. To the inventor of this useful machine the grain grower will ever feel grateful.

In all these tasks the women shared equally with the men. They helped to gather the stumps, and to burn the piles. They bound, stooked, and stacked grain. They sheared the sheep and washed the wool beside those pleasant little brooks, that ran through almost every farm. The water used was warmed in iron boilers brought from Scotland.

For many years threshing was done with the flail. This instrument consisted of two hardwood bars loosely tied together at the ends by a thong, preferably of buckskin. The handle was longer than the swingle to prevent the latter hitting the hand clasping the handle. Two parallel rows of six sheaves each, were laid on the barn floor with heads together and bands uncut. These were beaten with the flail until the straw began to curl. Then they were turned over with the flail, and the same punishment administered to the other side. The straw was stored for fodder and bedding. The grain was thrown into the air to separate it from the chaff. The lightest and cleanest chaff was carefully preserved to fill the home-made linen ticks on which the hard worked pioneers spent their all-too-few hours of hard earned rest.

The horse tread-mill consigned the flail to museum walls. The open cylinders first used were studded with hardwood teeth. The straw was passed back with hand rakes and forks and stored in the loft. After the evening meal was over the threshers returned to the barn. In an atmosphere clogged with dust, they put through the fanners all grain threshed that day. There seems to have been less opposition to the introduction of the fanners into Belfast than into Peel County, Ontario, where a certain lady tried to expel from the church a neighbor who had brought into the district one of those "wind machines."

Persistent cropping without rotation, soon impoverished the soil to such an extent that the yield was reduced by half. To restore fertility, farmers within a radius of several miles hauled "mussel mud" from Orwell River. This was thrown in small heaps over the field and in summer scattered in a thin layer. The digger was set up on the ice over an oyster bed. Those engaged were protected from the bitter winter winds by spruce trees planted in the ice, about the machine. An iron shovel worked by horse capstan, was lowered through an opening in the ice to scoop up and deposit in the sleigh the slimy mass of shells. To the humble oyster much of the prosperity and consequent happiness of the Island is due. Among the many resources with which it is so bountifully blessed this inconspicuous bivalve will ever hold an honored place.

Wooden ploughs with wrought iron mould-board, share, and colter, were long in use. In the earliest models the share and mould-board were in one piece. These were later made of cast iron in separate sections.

Stump fences were never a distinctive feature of Island landscape. Soft fir and spruce grew in abundance, and as they were easily cut the fences were made of them. The rails, or "longers" as they were known, were generally twelve feet long. These fences were built five rails high, then staked. A rider was placed over the stakes.

The wedding was often a day of jollification. The men present engaged in feats of physical prowess, running, jumping, throwing the heavy hammer, shooting at targets, and other Highland games.

It was customary for her parents to *tocher* the bride with a milk cow, a few sheep, and bedding for one bed. In the evening dancing was continued until, with great show and much burlesque, the assembled guests assisted the newly wedded pair to bed.

As the evening wore to its close a group of young men from the neighborhood armed with shot guns, tin pans, circular saws, horns, bugles, and other noise producing instruments, gathered outside the wedding house for the charivari. Here they kept up a continual din until, spent with their exertions, they accepted the invitation of the kindly host to share in the good things on the banquet table, or received from the groom a gift of money, which, as sometimes happened, they spent at the nearest tavern before going home.

Dances were usually held in the winter. A favorite time was at "house warmings," and sometimes at weddings. The Plain Quadrille, Scotch Reel, Step Dance, and Highland Schottische were the favorites. Another favorite was Sir Roger De Coverly, also known as the Virginia Reel.

The musical instrument generally used was the fiddle, but in default of it the mouth organ and jews-harp were sometimes used. One talented old lady with an ear for music, delighted her audience with strains from a coarse-tooth comb covered with thin paper. She used to be in great demand at these dances.

Much of the enjoyment at these gatherings was due to the "caller off." He was responsible for the movement of the various figures, and was often chosen because of special capacity to provoke merriment. In loud tones heard above the hum of conversation and the noise of shuffling feet, he called off the well remembered litany:

> Salute your partner—corner lady—
> First four right and left—
> Balance four—
> Turn partners
> Ladies, chain
> Chain back and half promenade—
> Half right and left to place—

It sometimes happened that the young men and women were present in unequal numbers. The genial caller-off, or perhaps some wag, to add a note of mirth, often varied the ritual by calling "swing or cheat." At this some hapless swain quickly stepped between a dancing lady and her partner and cheated him out of his swing. This sometimes provoked a jealous suitor to reprisals. On one occasion an aspiring youth tried to cheat, but for his pains his ears were boxed soundly by the indignant young lady who would have nothing to do with him.

Mrs. Alexander Gillis of Kinross, was born on the farm of her father, Donald Ban Oig MacLeod, beside the Orwell Head church, over eighty years ago. When recently questioned about amusements in the Orwell district of her youth, she declared without hesitation that, while geese raffles and other gatherings provided much fun for the young people, the wauking, or "thickening frolic" was the happiest day of the year.

These frolics were common in the winter time. When the web of cloth, containing generally from fifteen to thirty yards, according to the needs of the family, was ready for thickening, word was sent through the settlement. When those who wished to do so had assembled, the web, which had been soaking for some time in soap and water, was "wrung out" by hand. It was then placed on a long table improvised from boards placed on barrels. The young women lining each side of the table then grasped the cloth in their hands, at the same time giving a kneading movement as they advanced along and around it. This was accompanied by a Gaelic song, the rhythm of which lent itself to the movement. The hilarity produced by the singing robbed the task of any appearance or sense of labor. After repeated manipulations the cloth became quite thick. It was then rolled tightly on a wooden roller and allowed to stand for a few days. From this it was rolled off onto another roller and allowed to stand for a short time. When removed it was perfectly smooth and ready to be tailored by the women or by the community tailor, who was recognized as an important personage in the district. He went from house to house as his work called him.

Following the thickening, the evening was spent in step dancing and reels. When instrumental music was lacking a jigger chanted his wavering melody to the amusement and great delight of the whole party. Some of these jiggers had a ready fund of humorous anecdotes and an uncanny gift of mimicry. They were always welcome guests and did much to improve an evening.

At this early period the reel and step dance were the only ones she ever saw. Mrs. Gillis believes that for the first generation the Belfast people never danced the quadrille. It came into favor later.

The Gaelic songs most often sung around the thickening table were:

Mo Roighinn s'mo Run (The Choice of My Heart).

Thainig An Gille Dubh (My Laddie Came to This Town).

Oran Luaigh (Walking Song).

Songs were composed to commemorate striking events in the district. Some were in Gaelic, others in English. One of the most popular of the latter was "The Belfast Riot." The authorship is in doubt, but it gives a fairly complete history of that exciting event. It consisted of twelve stanzas. The first two were: —

The Belfast Riot

Come, brethren all, lend an ear to my story,
And naught but the truth unto you will I tell,
Concerning a fight that's recorded in story,
And of that brave hero who on that day fell.
Yon place in Belfast, with lilt and claymore
The old sons of Scotia in plenty were found,
With thistle and lion and bright banner flying,
And piper's long streamer and pibrochs resound.

The first of March was the day of election,
And the year forty-seven I heard them all say,
The Irish assembled from every direction,
Each one with his weapon concealed in
  his sleigh,
To drive from the hustings with cudgel well
  shapen
All who for brave Donald should vote on
  that day,
But that day, three to one, they were sadly
  mistaken
Our noble Scotch heroes made them all
  run away.

During the long winter evenings young and
old gathered in neighboring homes to "ceilidh,"
drawn by the genial atmosphere that pervades
certain homes in every community. There they
told stories and sang folk-songs. These were in
Gaelic, and among them, according to Roderick
C. MacLeod, the Gaelic scholar of Dundee, the
favorites, all brought from the Homeland, were:

   Fhir A' Bhata (O, My Boatman).
   Cabar Feidh (Clan Song of Seaforth Mackenzies).
   An Gleann' San Robh Mi'og (The Glen Where
     I was Young).
   Oidche Mhath Leibh (Good Night-Parting Song).
   Posadh Puithir Ian Bhain (Highland

Wedding Song).

Horo Mo Nighean Donn Ohoidheach (My Nut-Brown Maiden).

Bu Chaomh Leum Bhi Mirreadh (My Young Brunette).

Bha Mi'n Raoir An Coille Chaoil (Last Night in the Hazel Wood).

Mo Run Geal Dileas (My Faithful Fair One).

Cumha Mhic Criomain (MacCrimmon's Lament).

Between 1827, when Dr. Macauley died, and 1840, when Donald Munro, of Alberry Plains, arrived from Skye, there was no one in the district trained in medicine. During that period each district had one or more unselfish neighbors of practical skill, who prescribed simple remedies for the various ailments. Through their intelligent interest and devoted care many lives were saved, but the death toll from tuberculosis, diphtheria, scarlet fever, croup, pneumonia, and epidemics that frequently swept over the country, was heavy. These men did valuable work, but the midwives of Belfast exhibited a skill beyond all praise. They were equal to every emergency. They never turned a deaf ear to a call for help and without thought of reward they braved miles of miserable roads and bitter storms. Finally, when they made way for the modern practitioner, they left behind a record of unselfish care and skill, rarely, if ever, equalled under similar circumstances.

To every school boy the sea captain is a hero. In the fall of the year the docks were lined with ships loading cargoes of the famed McIntyre potatoes, or the equally famed black oats. The summit of the young boy's desire was gratified if permitted to bring a discarded whisky bottle full of milk to proffer the captain for the privilege of inspecting the hidden mysteries of the ocean Leviathan. Returning home, the assembled family heard of the wonders seen—the captain's cabin with its reeky lamp, the tiny sweating forecastle, and the cavernous hold in which was spied the dripping puncheon of Barbadoes molasses, nectar destined for the children's daily porridge.

These sailors were courageous, stern men. Inured to hardship and facing danger as their daily lot, they were disciplined and self controlled. If, in moments of dire peril, the mate's voice boomed above the fury of the storm, it was not a characteristic of the sailor. The same man, especially if a Highland Scot, was urbane ashore, speaking in that quiet undertone that is recognized as a characteristic peculiar to all sailors, and also one marking the speech of all the inhabitants of that beloved isle.

For the first sixty or seventy years of the settlement's existence there were notable fishing grounds stocked with a plentiful supply of cod, herring and mackerel within a few miles of their homes. To these grounds the young men used frequently to go for a few weeks, each summer. Erecting huts on St. Peter's Island they made it their headquarters, and did a thriving business with American shipowners who used to buy their catch. Unfortunately, these grounds no longer provide this near source of pleasure and profit to the people.

Among the few Lowland families who settled among the Highlanders, and taught them improved methods of farming, were the Andersons of Orwell Cove, who emigrated from Perth, Scotland, in 1808 to New Perth, P.E.I., and settled in Orwell Cove about 1819. They were, like most Lowlanders, more thrifty than the Highlanders. About 1842 or 1843 Alexander Anderson II built up-to-date mills on the Newtown River to which people carried grain from long distances.

The first iron plough in the district was brought from Scotland by Alexander Anderson I. He also brought the first cart wheels, and gig, and what did even more for the prosperity of the community, the famous black oats. All he grew for years was sold to the neighbors for seed. The daughters in this splendid family were equally as notable as the sons. Their skill in husbandry and in the domestic arts, made them outstanding women.

The heckle they brought from Scotland, was the first used in Orwell Cove. They taught their neighboring Highland women not only how to use it, but also how to plant and harvest the flax on which to use it.

Another Lowland family of unusual parts was the Irving family of Vernon River. From the first they exhibited those sterling qualities of thrift, industry and originality that inspired others and made them leaders in the district since first they entered it.

The First Mill in Belfast

The mills were among the most important factors ministering to the comfort of the early settlers. Each favorable stream had one or more. The first mill in Belfast was built by Lord Selkirk on the Pinette River near the church. Various parties operated it until finally, in 1839, John Douse sold it to Alexander Dixon, a miller from Bowport, Northumberland, England, whose grandson, Joseph Dixon, owns and operates it today in keeping with the fine tradition handed down through succeeding generations of that worthy family.

Oatmeal was ground in it for several years before the first wheat flour was made. In addition to the grist and saw-mill originally built, both carding and shingle mills were added at an early date. Prior to the installation of the carding mill, probably by Mr. Dixon, wool was carded in the settlers' homes by small wooden cards studded with iron bristles. Holding the handle of the card, which was about five inches by eight inches or ten inches, in each hand the wool was pulled and rolled into the required form for spinning.

THE KIRK

The Belfast settlers, like their kinsmen of the Red River Settlement, for many years were without a settled minister. They regarded this as a heavy cross, but bore it with patience. They longed to have observed, in the form they loved, the sacred rite of baptism, of marriage, and the final rites at death. They looked forward eagerly to the day when, in Gaelic, they might hear in their own church the voice of their own minister. For this day many waited in vain. At last in 1823 there was sent to minister to them the much revered John MacLennan. In the meantime the observance of religion was not neglected, and nothing shows more clearly their reverence for the Sabbath than their strict observance of that day.

The church was the lodestone around which centred the life of the people. Young and old alike presented themselves at divine service clothed in their best, and comported themselves in a manner befitting the sacred nature of the service. There was no endowment, but all reasonable demands were met. The people contributed willingly of what they had. The minister's stipend may seem trifling today, but it was adequate at that time. He was easily able to support himself and family in a manner befitting his station. No one was rich and it was proper that he should not have luxuries while his parishioners dined on humble fare. There was thus complete fellowship in the community.

There is a tradition in Belfast that John Gillis, a Skyeman who settled in Orwell Cove in 1803, built a log structure near the French cemetery, probably in 1804, which for years was used both for church and for school. It is believed that Dr. Aeneas Macaulay, who had been an army chaplain before studying medicine, frequently conducted religious service during the early years of the settlement in that building, and also in private homes.

The church records seem to indicate that the present church was erected in 1823, where it now stands, near Pinette River, on land granted for the purpose by Selkirk; but it is held by some that it was built in 1824. It is an imposing and beautiful structure, a tribute alike to the high value put upon spiritual things by the early settlers, and to their unbounded confidence in the future of their settlement. They had early taken firm root in the new land. With the speedy improvement in their financial condition their contentment grew apace, and no regrets were felt over their migration from the home of their forefathers. The building is sixty feet long by forty-two feet wide. The Wren steeple is composed of a tower fourteen feet wide by sixteen feet long, surmounted by a spire of unusual beauty eighty-five feet high. The spire was built by the two brothers, Neil MacLeod and Malcolm MacLeod (father of Donald Mor MacLeod of Orwell). They had both worked in the U.S.A., and after returning to their old home at Murray Harbor Road, about 1860, erected the spire. There is a gallery on both sides and one end.

Up to the time the church was built and for a couple of generations later, shingles were made by hand from the choicest wood, free from knots. The instrument used in making them—the "frow"—had a wedge-shaped iron blade about a foot long attached to which was a short stout handle. The block of wood was stood on end and the "frow" driven by a wooden mallet into the end of the block so as to give the shingle, or barrel stave, as the case might be, the required thickness. With the block braced against the knee, the handle was then pulled sideways and the required piece split off. The piece thus severed followed the grain of the wood.

This was then planed by hand. The result was a shingle which endured until completely worn off by the elements. The shingles now on the churches at Belfast, Orwell and Orwell Head are of this variety. In the former case, although exposed to the elements for almost three quarters of a century, they are still sound.

It is not known when the first bell was hung, but it was cracked in the collapse of the belfry, and sent to England to be recast. The one now in the tower is inscribed "St. John's Church, 1834." Whether it was paid for by the parishioners or not is uncertain, but there is a tradition among the older living residents that one of the early governors had something to do with it. The site is one of surpassing beauty. On a high hill, surrounded by a grove of beautiful maples, the church, which has stood for over one hundred years, commands one of the finest prospects in the whole province. It is a constant reminder to those who worship in it, of the discernment and discretion of those farseeing ancestors who chose the spot, so many years ago, and who now, their life work ended, sleep in hallowed peace in the little graveyard surrounding it on all sides. Perhaps no church in the whole province has so much of interesting history and romance enshrined in its annals as the famous old Belfast church. Ministering to a congregation extending around it to a distance of five or six miles, it has known over a century of active prosperity and of inestimable usefulness.

In a copy of the Monthly Record of the Church of Scotland in Nova Scotia, and the adjoining Provinces, for October, A.D. 1864, in the possession of Miss Bella Macdonald, postmistress, Eldon, Belfast, appears the following, written no doubt by the minister:

St. John's Church, Belfast

"This church, one of the oldest buildings among our places of worship, is now undergoing a thorough renovation. At a meeting of the Congregation held a few weeks ago, it was resolved to make extensive repairs, so as to secure comfort and the respectability of appearance which should distinguish everywhere the House of God. A large and very liberal subscription was made on the spot, and although but a few weeks have passed since the work was resolved on, a large portion of it has already been accomplished. Before the end of October the whole will be finished, and it includes, besides other necessary repairs and changes, the shingling and plastering of the whole building, with the addition of a large vestry.

"This church, when originally built about forty years ago, was one of the best of the Protestant churches in the Island. It is now again about to resume its original position, and to become what the church occupied by a congregation like that of Belfast should be. In the meantime, and for some weeks to come, public worship must be held in the open air, which, although not always very comfortable, is cheerfully submitted to by pastor and people, from the pleasure and comfort anticipated when again permitted to occupy the sacred building. To complete these extensive repairs will require an amount of upwards of £250. A short time ago, another church was erected at Orwell, for the accommodation of that section of the congregation residing there, at a cost exceeding £300. This has been done amid difficulties caused by an almost entire failure in the crops. For two successive seasons they were subjected to this severe trial, and the debts then incurred in providing food for themselves and families still continue to embarrass many of them. The efforts which, in these circumstances, have thus been made, and the vigour with which especially this last one is being carried on, speak well for our people, and afford some evidence that they value the means of grace."

(Signed) A Belfaster.

Following the above article is an account of a presentation to Rev. Alexander Maclean, the able and highly respected minister of the Belfast congregation, of a set of silver mounted harness and whip, gift of a number of gentlemen of the congregation. The address is reproduced. It is signed by the following committee on behalf of the donors:

John Macleod, Elder.
James Nicholson, Elder.
Daniel Fraser, Major.
Donald Macleod.
William Maclean.
Joseph M. Dixon.
George Young, Junior.

The minister's lengthy reply, dated August 22nd, 1864, is also given.

The Belfast church was thoroughly repaired again in 1922. Mr. R. E. Macdonald, of Pinette, Secretary-Treasurer of the congregation, in a letter dated May 21, 1927, reports as follows:

"The first foundation of the Belfast church was stone blocks, which, after ninety-nine years of service, were, in 1922, as good as new, but not high enough for present needs. We raised the whole building twenty-eight inches, and replaced the stone blocks with concrete, enlarged the cellar, built a new vestry, replaced the two small windows in the east end with one large one, installed two new pipeless furnaces, shingled one side of roof with cedar, and affixed new eaves to the main building. Many people considered it impossible to raise this building, it was done in three hours by forty-eight men, and an equal number of jack screws and several other helpers. It was a memorable day to see this beautiful and historic building with its high tower and two large chimneys raised so easily without crack or break of any kind. The jacks cost 50 cents each per day, and the men $2.00 per day.

"The total cost of the work was $3,856.01. Of this sum $3,161.49 was paid out in cash, whilst $694.52 was given in voluntary labor.

"In the summer of 1926 we painted the whole structure and attached new eaves on the tower at a cost of about $550.00.

"The cemetery, which was heretofore managed by a Committee, is now under the control of the Board of Trustees, who are going to make an effort to maintain the sacred spot in that degree of respectability pleasing to all who have loved ones interred in it."

THE CEMETERIES

"Again I behold where for hours I have
  ponder'd,
As reclining, at eve, on yon tombstone I lay;
Or round the steep brow of the churchyard
  I wander 'd.
To catch the last gleam of the sun's setting ray."

Although the French cemetery, situated on the McMillan farm near Halliday's Wharf, was used as their first burial-ground, a new one was soon established at Mount Buchanan. There Dr. Angus Macaulay set aside a parcel of land from his estate for a cemetery, and there that good man was buried. This burial-ground was called *Cleachd an' leighaich* (the Doctor's burying-ground).

The first person buried in it was one of the Doctor's infant children. It continued to be used by many families for years after the new churchyard beside the church was opened, and is used by some families today.

On the Macaulay tombstone in the Mount Buchanan burying-ground is the following inscription:

In Memory of
ANGUS MACAULAY, M.D.,
Chaplain of H. Majesty's First West
India Regiment.
He settled Belfast with emigrants from
Scotland in the memorable ship
"Polly" in 1803. He died Dec. 6,
1827, aged 67 years.

Also his wife, Mary, died April 9,
1857, aged 99, daughter of Samuel
McDonald, of Sartle, Scotland, Capt. in
H. Majesty's Army during the
American Revolution.

The first person interred in the burial-ground
about the Belfast church was, according to some,
Mr. Beaton of Flat River, while others aver it was
John Gillis of Orwell Cove. Almost as early must
have been the following, to whose memory existing stones bear witness:

ALEX. MACKENZIE
died Feb. 28, 1824, aged 76.

ANGUS MCMILLAN,
died December 16, 1824, aged 54.
Native of Skye.

The French cemetery is today in a neglected and ruinous condition. On October 21, 1928, there was one headstone only standing erect in this historic cemetery. Of Wallace freestone, it bore in legible characters the following inscription:

In Memory of
ALEXANDER NICHOLSON,
A native of Skye, Invernesshire, who
departed this life 26 September, 1820,
aged 40 years.
His wife Mary Nicholson, who died
3rd May, 1854, aged 65 years.
And their daughter Isabella, who died
November 16, 1844, aged 25.

In the same cemetery two months earlier, there stood erect, in good repair, a marble stone inscribed as follows.

In Memory of
DONALD MARTIN,
departed this life July 1, 1861,
Aet 78. Emigrated to this Island 1803.
And our souls are in eternal rest,
For our bodies are here asleep,
Dear friend for us do not weep.
Also his wife Ann, departed this life
April 8, 1850, Aet 65.

In the intervening two months this stone had been thrown down and broken, leaving as sole watchman to mark the last resting place of sharers in an experiment noble in its philanthropy, but one poor slab of stone. Sleeping in the old graveyard beside the church are many whose careers at the time aroused interest and curiosity, and whose characters now evoke admiration.

Harriet Campbell, daughter of Hugh Campbell, Killundin, Marvin, Argyleshire, married one Allan Macdougall, and in the early history of Belfast, settled at Flat River. She is said to have been connected with the noble house of Argyle. Her early training unfitted her for the pioneer life of Belfast, and existence there was a sore trial to her. Her proud spirit and dauntless courage surmounted every obstacle, and although suffering great hardships she refused to leave the land of her adoption. She died on November 10, 1863, at Union Road, Lot 51, aged 70, and was buried in Belfast churchyard.

The late Mrs. Donald Ross, of Kinross, lived beside them as a young girl, and recalled late in life how they stood for courtesy and refinement in an age and situation when the outward expression of those virtues was difficult. Mr. MacDougall was not suited to the environment in which he lived. Incapable of earning with his hands, there was no outlet for his talents. "If only there was someone to talk with!" was the plaintive cry uttered by his superior and finely educated consort, pining in the isolated forest of the new land for old friends and the culture of the homeland. When one of her neighbors urged her, in her distress, to write to her brother for aid, she proudly replied "Never, I will die first." And so Harriet Campbell, scion of one of Europe's noblest and most distinguished houses, suffered and endured, and finally met her end with unflinching courage. Old residents even yet recall many interesting stories of this proud and highly educated couple, and the hardship they endured in the rude surroundings in which they were placed.

More tragic still was the case of Lord Selkirk's only daughter Mary. She was placed by the Earl in care of Thomas Halliday, a skilled Scottish stonemason of good education and excellent character. When he and his family arrived in Belfast in 1806, accompanied by their adopted child, then seven years of age, he was given a farm near the present Halliday's Wharf. Mary was also dowered with certain adjoining lands. At an early age she married a son of her foster parents. Descendants of this union, Hallidays, McLennans, McTavishes, and others still live in this district, and are highly respected.

A tombstone in the old Belfast churchyard marks the grave of Mary, daughter of the Earl of Selkirk:

In loving memory of
Mary Douglas,
only daughter of Lord Selkirk, died
October, 1859, Aet 60.
Blessed are the dead,
Who die in the Lord.
Erected by her daughter,
E. McLennan.

In 1904, to mark the centenary of the founding of the Belfast district, the descendants of the pioneers and their friends, at the entrance to the graveyard around Belfast church, erected a monument bearing the following inscription, with one in Gaelic to the same effect:

In Memory
of the arrival of the Scottish Immigrants
who came to this Island by Lord Selkirk's
ships, The Polly, Dykes and Oughton, in
August, 1803, and made homes for
themselves and their children in the woods
of Belfast.

According to the records of the Belfast congregation, now in the possession of Mr. R. E. Macdonald of Pinette, the following were the ministers of the Congregation:

Rev. John Maclennan—September 1823 to September 1849 (Aberdeen).

Rev. Alexander MacKay—August 1855 to June 1859 (Univ. in Scotland, unknown).

Rev. Alexander MacLean—August 1859 to September 1877 (Glasgow, D.D. Pine Hill).

Rev. Alexander Sinclair Stewart—March 1879 to January 1887 (D.D. Pine Hill).

Rev. Alexander MacLean Sinclair—May 1888 to June 1906 (D.D. Pine Hill, LL.D. St. François Xavier).

Rev. Samuel D. MacPhee—November 1906 to December 1909 (B.A. Dal.—Pine Hill).

Rev. James W. MacKenzie—July 1910 to July 1925 (B.A. Dal. Mont. Pres. Coll.)

Rev. T. A. Rodger—June 1928. Present incumbent.

Mr. Maclennan was born in the Highlands of Scotland in 1797, and is believed to have graduated from Aberdeen University. He was sent by the Church of Scotland to Prince Edward Island to minister to the emigrants from the Highlands and Islands of Scotland who had settled in various parts of the Island, the largest number being in Belfast. He preached in Georgetown, Wood Islands, Murray Harbor, and occasionally in Charlottetown, Cherry Valley and New London. When he arrived in 1823 the first and only Protestant clergyman on the island was Rev. Theophilus DesBrisay.

The manse was not ready, and perhaps it was not even started, when the new minister and his wife[1] arrived. For the first few months at least, they were guests of Hector Mackenzie, Flat River. Mrs. Maclennan brought her piano with her. It may be assumed that for many long years it was the only instrument of the kind in the whole countryside. The house was small and there was difficulty in getting it through the narrow hall to a room. It is hard to imagine today what this piano must have meant to the neighbors.

The few now living who knew her testify to the beauty, charm and happy disposition of Mrs. Maclennan. The moral ascendancy acquired by her husband during the course of his ministry in Belfast, was due in no small measure to the talented and wise companion who brought so much sunshine into the life of the parish.

The stipend was a matter of indifferent speculation to the minister. He never knew what he would get, and cared less. Those who could pay in cash gave what they could afford. Those who had no money, and they were in the majority, contributed freely from their store of potatoes, meat, butter, eggs, fish and such other

---

1   Catherine McNab, died Oct. 24, 1890, aged 86.

farm products as they raised.

In sickness he helped the afflicted with simple remedies, and on more than one occasion he nursed patients through their critical illness. He settled differences and promoted harmony. Many a disputed line was rectified according to the just decision of that wise man. He drew their wills and advised in business affairs. His sympathy was so wide and his understanding so deep that he became the trusted friend and beloved companion of the whole community. Over them all his influence was unchallenged and supreme. Finally, after years of arduous toil he felt the need of rest and change. The grief expressed by men and women alike, as in 1849 he passed along the road on his way to visit his native land, never to return, was long remembered by those who shared it. Each family waited at the gate to bid a fond farewell, men, women, and children in tears.

One of their three striking and talented daughters married Daniel Miner Gordon, for many years the Principal of Queen's University, Kingston, Ontario.

While yet a mere child, one of the daughters of Rev. Mr. and Mrs. Maclennan met a tragic end. Following her nurse, who had gone to a neighbors, she got mired in attempting to cross the then exposed river flats. The incoming tide engulfed her. When it had receded her body was recovered from the slimy river bottom where she had sunk beyond her frail power to release herself.

> "Kilmeny looked up with a lovely grace.
> But nae smile was seen on Kilmeny's face;
> As still was her look, and as still was her e'e,
> As the stillness that lay on the emerant lea,
> Or the mist that sleeps on a waveless sea."

The following inscription is on a monument erected to his memory in the Belfast churchyard:

Sacred
To the Memory of
The REV. JOHN MACLENNAN,
who died at Kilchernnan, Scotland, on
the 11th February, 1852, aged 55
years. He was the first minister of this
congregation, being settled in 1822
and for 26 years amidst trials and
difficulties laboured unweariedly in his
Master's service.

and within the church is a tablet, placed by a descendant of one of his parishioners, on which is inscribed:

To the Memory of
REV. JOHN MACLENNAN,

First Minister of this Church
Born in Ross-shire, Scotland, in 1797,
died in Argyleshire, Scotland, 1852.
He served this parish from 1823 to
1849, a period of 26 years. He was
a beloved and faithful servant of the Lord.

Mr. Mackay is believed also to have been born
and educated in Scotland.

Mr. Maclean was born in Pictou County, Nova
Scotia, and died there a few years ago. His first
wife was Miss Matheson from Pictou County, N.S.
His second wife was Matilda Brown, from Charlottetown, a lady highly esteemed and beloved
by the congregation.

Mr. Stewart was born in Tiree, Scotland. This
kindly, lovable pastor, after leaving Belfast, ministered in adjoining parishes until a few years
ago. He now lives at Montague Bridge, P.E.I., in
retirement, enjoying the respect and affection
earned by a long life of unselfish labor devoted
to helping others.

Mr. Sinclair was a nephew of his predeces-
sor, Mr. Maclean, and came from Nova Scotia,
a province which has given Sir William Dawson,
Simon Newcomb, and many other illustrious
men to our country. Mr. Sinclair in later life lec-
tured on Celtic language and literature, in Pine
Hill College, Halifax, and Saint François Xavier

University, Antigonish, N.S., a subject on which
he was regarded by many at the time as the greatest living authority. He died a few years ago. A
son, Donald M. (B. A. Dal.; Ph.D. Edin.), is now
minister in Valleyfield, P.E.I.

Mr. Macphee, a son of Donald Macphee, miller
of Heatherdale, and his wife Margaret, daughter
of Donald Nicholson, miller of Orwell, was the
first descendant of a pioneer of Belfast to become
minister of the parish. He died in Ontario a few
years ago.

Mr. Mackenzie lives in retirement in Charlottetown.

Mr. Rodger, the present minister, was born in
Kingston, Ontario.

Although Belfast has been notable for the high
character of her ministers, all the clergy who
labored on Prince Edward Island were not saints.
Some were very human and exhibited traces of
those less amiable qualities that one more often
looks for in the laity. One of these gentlemen
possessed to an unusual extent the desire, and
developed to an artistic degree, the art of teasing,
not only his fellow men, but members of the lower
animal kingdom as well.

On one occasion, arising from morning prayer
with the faithful adherents whom he was visiting,
he said to a member of the household gathered
around, "Did you notice the dig I gave John in my
prayer?" Later, on going from the house to the

barn yard, he met the lord of the sheepfold. Mutual antagonism at once declared itself. To meet the oncoming rush the clergyman raised a heel, and as the dazed ram passed beneath the unstable object of his attack, the clergyman wheeled about to receive a second charge in the same spot. Thus the battle raged, until, amazed and confounded, the bellicose guardian of the barnyard had spent his baffled fury in futile rushes and shaking of head. By mutual, if silent, consent a truce was declared, and the woolly champion of his flock withdrew to his seraglio, whilst the shepherd of his flock betook himself to his books.

Power of the Kirk

After the Reformation in Scotland the power of the Kirk was very great, and in the exercise of discipline it was very strict. As the Belfast settlers were Presbyterian they naturally brought with them their Church polity. But the atmosphere of North America was not the atmosphere of Scotland. The result was that the exercise of Church discipline was greatly relaxed. In Scotland such offences as drunkeness, blasphemy, profaning the Sabbath, cursing, swearing, absenting oneself from hearing the Word, Examination and Sacrament of the Holy Supper, and other offences rendered

the accused liable to be brought before the Kirk
Session, where evidence was heard and weighed.
The ordinary penalty for general offences was for
the guilty party to stand in the Kirk door clothed
in sackcloth or in linen, barefoot and bareheaded,
and later within the church to confess his guilt.
In the presence of the congregation he was then
solemnly rebuked. It is true that in the early days
of Belfast church accused persons, on more than
one occasion, had to submit to the humiliation of
public interrogation for their delinquencies, but
although severely and solemnly rebuked, at no
time was anyone ever pursued with the harshness
that characterized similar investigations in the
land of their forefathers.

It is also to the credit of this community that,
although there have always been witches in their
midst, no one has ever in its history been tried for
witchcraft, sorcery, divination, or fortune telling.
But the functions of the Kirk-Session in Belfast
were not treated lightly, either by themselves or
by the members of the community, over whose
morals and general conduct they had by long
recognized usage a power of investigation. The
prospect of moral delinquency being publicly
exposed and condemned by this ecclesiastical
Witenagemote of long-bearded grave gentlemen,
had a deterrent effect that, at least in the early
days of the colony, must have strengthened the

moral purpose of those who feared the condemnation and social ostracism of their friends, more than they craved the pleasures derived from the pursuit of what their less rigid successors would call innocent pleasures.

The semi-circle of austere elders before the pulpit was visible warning to all potential backsliders that condign punishment might still be meted out to those whose conduct fell below church standards as interpreted by them.

But there was another side to the character of these stern men. If they seemed hard on occasions, they could be, and often were, tender. Their kindness to the lower forms of animal life in particular was striking.

It often seemed as if it were touched with the spirit of fatalism. They believed firmly in a special guiding Providence, and any indication of the Divine hand was treated as personal, and was not to be ignored.

On one occasion, at a meeting of the elders of the Murray Harbor Road church, during the incumbency of Rev. Donald Macdonald, a complaint was lodged on behalf of some of the worshippers, that their minds were distracted during the sacred services by the twitterings of swallows nesting in the chimneys. Finally Mr. William Macphail was asked to "go on." Standing up before the assembled elders, and taking in his hands the ponderous Bible that was resting on the table, he allowed it to fall open where it would. It was understood that the chapter thus exposed to view was the one Divinely appointed to be read. When he had finished the lines "Yea, the sparrow hath found an house, and the swallow a nest for herself, where she may lay her young, even thine Altars, O Lord of Hosts, my King, and my God," the fate of the swallows was settled. After a brief prayer was said the meeting was dispersed. Until these cheerful visitors betook themselves to a sunnier home in the south their merry twittering was a part of each service as unfailing as the reading of Holy Writ itself.

Looking back over the great part the elders played in the Presbyterian Church of early days, one cannot but be amazed at their profound knowledge of Scripture. It almost seemed as if they knew the Bible from cover to cover. Did the minister fail to appear there was always an elder capable of expounding the Word with a fullness of allusion and wealth of illustration that would put to shame the modern college-bred clergyman.

The elders trained under Rev. Donald Macdonald were singularly well equipped in this regard, and that master often met his match in the elders' semi-circle before his pulpit.

Those who have listened to the public prayers of the elders, and of other disciples of Rev. Mr.

Macdonald, will never forget the matchless display of apt Bible quotation pouring forth in fine periods, with equal fluency in their beloved native Gaelic, or in their adopted English.

Reverend Samuel Angus Martin, now of Manitoba, recalls the occasion when, as a young man, he heard the debate between the elders of the Murray Harbor Road church as to whether "Cook's Helps" should be introduced into the Sunday school. Mr. William Macphail spoke in favor of the innovation. Ewen Lamont, a local preacher, arose and condemned the proposal. He made a speech filled with deep emotion. Finally, taking one of the pamphlets in his hands, and holding it aloft, he exclaimed with great feeling as he tore it asunder, "This is the human help to aid the Bible you would introduce into the Sunday school."

At the home of his father Samuel Martin, of Uigg, family worship was being conducted by Alexander MacEachern, of Millview. Before the service was commenced Mr. MacEachern turned all pictures in the room face to the wall, and put out the cat and dog. He recalls another occasion in the same house when the same gentleman was conducting worship. While he was praying the chimney caught fire. All the men and boys in the room went to help extinguish the blaze. The roof was scaled and salt and water applied to the roaring chimney. When the fire was finally extinguished and they returned to the room Mr. McEachern was still on his knees in prayer, exhibiting no outward show of emotion, or consciousness of the distraction that had driven others from the menaced house.

Mrs. Mary J. MacLeod, widow of Rev. D. B. MacLeod of Orwell, on the death of her father was adopted by her relative, Donald Joiner MacLeod, elder, of Kinross. Of the many customs which she recalls in this excellent household was that of the daily morning prayer. When Mr. MacLeod had the Bible ready, he called upon the women to cover their heads as enjoined by St. Paul: "Every woman that prayeth with her head uncovered dishonoreth her head" (Cor. 1, 2.). On these occasions the women present seized anything near at hand, such as an apron, men's hats, or any other object. On one occasion a lady visitor who was not aware of the customs of the house, on being offered a bonnet, replied "No thank you, my head is not cold."

Sunday Observance, Festivities, Drinking

There was the usual strong Presbyterian aversion to Sunday work and play. Anything tending to gaiety and happiness on that day was frowned upon as lacking in piety. Music and singing were restricted to that of a religious character. When the younger parishioners decided to instal, and did instal, an organ in the "Little" Church at Orwell cross-roads, there was great opposition on the part of a few of the more reactionary of the older generation at the ungodly innovation. This was as late as 1892. In as far as was possible provision was made on the previous day for the wants of the Sunday. Wood was prepared, water drawn, food cooked, all that a greater reverence might be shown the Almighty. These restrictions seem strange today, but the moral chastisement that followed their breach was a thing so potent that only the boldest dared defy.

Life among these Scots was a serious matter, and it was the studied intention and purpose of the older generation to keep it so.

The general atmosphere of the community was that there was an avenging God hovering over-head, or concealed in the adjoining forest, ever ready to pounce upon the guilty for breach of sacred or even profane duty. A sort of shadow hung over the moral atmosphere, which restrained and checked the natural flow of lively emotion and good spirits. The gaiety one usually finds in an English community was lacking.

Their pleasures and recreations were few. The times were hard. From infancy they knew self-denial and toil. Even the bare necessities of life were obtained only after fatiguing manual labor. It is not to be wondered at that their few and simple pleasures were taken almost sadly. Only under the spell of whisky did they entirely forget the sober hardships of a life of toil.

Their sombre outlook on life may have been due to qualities inherited from ancestors whose environment in a land of mist and mountain compelled an age-long struggle to force a bare living from unwilling nature.

Superstition was equally common among the Scots and Irish. In each there was a sensitive apprehension of the supernatural that is not found in the more logical English mind. The world about them seemed full of ghosts and fairies, and every unusual occurrence and dream had its mysterious significance. If a star were seen to fall, or a light to hover near a home, it presaged therein an early break in the family circle.

Living as they did in the woods, their surroundings were gloomy. The wind whistling through the dark forest, the crashing of falling trees, the foreboding shadows of the night, all added to their fear of Nature. As they sat around their hearth fire, listening to tales of warlocks and witches, their wildest fears were aroused. The fickle shadow from the pine knot dancing on the cabin wall assumed the form of hideous and malignant monsters waiting to lay cruel and avenging hands upon them. Although their intellect mocked their credulity, they were never able to free themselves entirely from the belief that there was a menacing force acting independent of the Natural and of the Divine.

The native honesty of the people manifested itself in their business relations. To ask for security for debt was unheard of. Promissory Notes were not in use, and refusal to honor an obligation was looked upon with great scorn.

Many of the Scots and Irish were hard drinkers. Public opinion did not then condemn drunkenness as it does today, and men were not ostracised for it. Rum was provided always at stumping frolics, and other such gatherings. Although ready money was scarce there seemed always to be a way to buy it in quantity on these occasions. No matter how great the supply the capacity of those in attendance seemed even greater. As long as the gathering consisted of neighbors there was no quarreling, but when the whole countryside assembled together, as at a "trot," as the horse race was called, there was occasion found by someone to break the peace, and several knots of men might be seen at the same time, in various places, circling around two or more half-drunken men, each of whom declared with oaths and curses that he was champion of Belfast.

Those living near taverns were scandalized frequently by shameful scenes of revelry. Drunken men reeled about the roads insulting, with profane and filthy language, and sometimes with physical assault, all whom they met.

Weddings were sometimes marked by unseemly conduct on the part of drinkers, and, strange as it may seem today, funerals likewise were seized upon by some as occasions for great license, but never to the same extent as the Irish wake. On one occasion there was a thickening frolic at the home of a resident of Orwell. To slake the thirst that seemed to seize everyone at such gatherings the head of the house started on foot for Eldon with an empty rum jar. A wild winter storm came up during the afternoon. Next morning friends seeking the missing one found his frozen body at the top of the hill near Orwell bridge, within a mile of home and safety.

The clergy of all denominations urged a more moderate use of alcohol. A change came about slowly, and today drinking to excess is a very rare occurrence.

In Father James Phalen, of Vernon River Parish, and his brother, Father William Phalen, of Montague Parish, the liquor interests had two notable opponents. Two more worthy or faithful servants of their church it would be difficult to find. Ever striving to help the lot of their parishioners, they were feared and respected leaders of their respective flocks.

Of the latter it is related that during a certain political and religious agitation, perhaps over the "Manitoba School Question," he made a memorable statement. An election was about to be held. He had just finished reading an episcopal message from the pulpit when he addressed his audience as follows: "And now, as in duty bound, I have read the message of my ecclesiastical superiors. As for myself, I mean to vote for Mr. Welsh on election day."

It need scarcely be said that Mr. William Welsh was the candidate of the Liberal party, against which the wrath of the hierarchy was directed.

Sacrament

Anyone who expressed a desire to formally unite with the church was personally examined as to his or her faith and conduct, by the minister and elders of the church, a few days before Sacramental Sunday. If it was found to the satisfaction of the examining board that the applicant was a person worthy to partake of the Sacrament, he was given a small paper ticket, called a "token," on which was printed the words, "This do in remembrance of Me." On Sunday, when Sacrament was being administered by the clergy, assisted by certain of the elders, the candidate could, on coming forward and giving up the token, receive the bread and wine. At this time individual cups were not in use. A few days before this event the "ruling" elder, or one of his brethren, drove to Charlottetown, and purchased the necessary wine from one of the dealers there. The people looked upon the occasion as a very solemn one, fraught with the possibility of much good or ill, depending on the uses made of the privileges of Grace thus so freely offered.

Sacrament was held once a year in June. Preparatory services were held in the forenoon of Friday and Saturday preceding the observance of that ordinance. At these services the minister was usually assisted by one, or more, clergymen, generally from adjoining parishes. At these services the people were encouraged to make a serious survey of their lives and to resolve on future conduct more in keeping with their privileges.

On Sunday morning the spectator might discern in the distance trailing clouds of dust that marked the approach of a great concourse of pilgrims, on every road leading to the church. Long before eleven o'clock, when the services were scheduled to begin, the sacred edifice was crowded to the doors, while outside, standing or seated on the grass, were many times the number inside. A movable pulpit, which was used for the same purpose from year to year, was provided for the clergy officiating outside. It was customary for the older people to worship in the church where the Sacrament was dispensed. Those taking it sat in the front seats, near the table on which the Bread and Wine were placed. After partaking of the symbols they withdrew to make way for others from outside. The parish minister usually conducted the service in the church, assisted sometimes by a minister from a neighboring parish, whose church was closed for that Sunday. The scene outside was one of extraordinary interest. Here was a minister in one of nature's beauty spots, addressing a gathering of romantic and pious Highlanders in their native tongue far from the land of their birth. The whole scene was such as to touch the tenderest and most responsive chords in the soul of this emotional people. About them were the graves and headstones that called to mind their dear departed. To the splendor of the overspreading trees was added the beauty of the verdant slope bedecked with buttercups and daisies, extending to the Pinette below. The fitful breeze wafted sounds of falling waters on the ear. The healing "balm of resinous gums," like incense, floated on the air. A sense of harmony pervaded the hallowed scene.

In such a setting the large congregation listened with bated breath to a rousing sermon in their beloved native Gaelic, and in the same language sang with lusty lungs the old familiar Hebrew Psalms.

The message was so fervid that time sped fast. When one o'clock was reached no one could justly charge their minister (as one of that order was once charged in Scotland) with being "so little serious and concerned, even when he is about immediate worship of God, that he hath been seen frequently, in the pulpit, to take out his watch and look what time of day it was."

When the service was over, the pious worshippers returned to their several homes refreshed, and with a feeling of exaltation derived from communion with spiritual things in surroundings made sacred by the blood of their fathers.

On the Monday morning following, the minister of the parish conducted a brief service that concluded the greatest annual religious and social event of the year in the life of the little parish, isolated in an out-of-the-way corner of the continent.

Settlement of Orwell

It is believed that the first settlers on the Orwell River were the Macdougalls and John Currie, all of whom took up land on the north bank. They were soon followed, in 1818, by the Macdonalds from Scotchfort, who had received their grant several years earlier.

On their way to their new home they blazed a trail from Head of Vernon River through Uigg to Orwell cross-roads, thereby establishing the course of the present Uigg road. Others soon followed, and when in 1821 the whole territory from Orwell bridge to Kinross was taken up by the MacLeods, Macdonalds and Rosses, the district had definitely emerged from the forest stage.

The marsh lands along the river were of great value to the early settler for pasture. Farmers came from miles around and cut the rank marsh grass with scythes. They built a "stance" on upright posts above the high water mark, and there they built their stacks. In the winter, when the marsh was frozen over, they hauled these stacks to their barns, where it was, for the early years of the settlement, the chief winter food for their cattle.

Wild geese, ducks, brant, upland plover, curlews, yellow legs, snipe, sand pipers, and other forms of wild game birds abounded to an extent that seems incredible today. Sea trout were also in abundance, as well as other varieties of excellent fish. Altogether it was a delightful spot.

About the same time Donald Nicholson moved to Orwell from Orwell Cove, and took up the farm through which the Orwell River winds for over a mile.

In the primeval forest a clearing was soon made. Margaret MacLeod (Peggy Neil), recalls the original dwelling house then built near the river on the north bank. It was a long, low, comfortable house of several rooms. Between it and the river was planted an orchard of cherry, plum, and apple trees. Later, in this house, modern wall-paper was used for the first time in the district, being then a great curiosity. For many years the family lived on this site. After the milling business went down, a home was built by a son, Peter, to the west of the road near the site of the present bridge, and beside a spring that still pours out its cooling waters.

Mills

About 1830 Donald Nicholson erected the first grist mill on this stream, near his dwelling house, about three or four hundred yards above the present Orwell bridge. It was built by William Harris, a skilled millwright from Devon, England, who later married the miller's daughter. A dwelling for the assistant miller was also built nearby. Today there is nothing to mark this scene of early activity, but the scarred hillside and the remains of the dam built to impound the waters. This grist mill was operated by him for many years, and for a few years by his son Peter, by his Highland neighbors commonly called "Patrick Stenscholl," from the locality in Skye where the family originated. Peter leased the mill to various tenants until it was finally abandoned.

William Gillis, aged 83, now living at Orwell bridge, worked in the mill as a young man with Mr. Maclean, a tenant. He recalls that large quantities of oatmeal were ground there at that time.

The flume was wide enough to permit vehicles to cross, and for many years it was used as the first public highway across Orwell River. Later, about 1840, a new bridge was built a few hundred yards farther down stream at the site of the present Orwell bridge.

A half mile above this mill was a saw-mill built and operated by George Gay from Lot 49, called by the Highland people *Gaieach Cam*, variously interpreted as reflecting on the physical eye or moral character. He had taken up the adjoining farm before 1829. His son, John Gay, afterwards occupied the farm and sold it to John Fletcher, who married Caroline, sister of James "Yankee" Hayden, of Vernon River. He, about 1840 or 1845, built a grist mill a few hundred yards farther up the stream. This mill subsequently passed into the possession of John F. MacLeod of Strathalbyn, brother of D. J. MacLeod, Superintendent of Education, who added a saw mill and operated it until a few years before his death in 1915, at seventy years of age.

A son of said John Fletcher, named James H. Fletcher, whose wife was Miss Moar from New Perth, after leaving Uigg school attended the Central Academy in Charlottetown about 1868. In 1869 he was editor of the *Island Argus*. From Charlottetown he moved to Pierre, South Dakota, of which State he was Lieutenant-Governor from 1889 to 1891. In the Western States he was recognized as an able orator, lecturer, and newspaper editor. From South Dakota he moved to Gresham, Oregon, where he lived for several years, until his death in 1910, over eighty years of age. His funeral service was conducted in that town by Rev. Malcolm C. Martin, son of Samuel Martin of Uigg, one of the neighbors and school companions of his youth.

Owing to economic changes, and the deaths of the various owners, the lower mills had been abandoned and the dams swept away, leaving in operation, only the mill highest up the stream. This continued until about 1910, when it, too, was abandoned and finally swept away by spring floods.

Some of the stones of the Nicholson mill were donated by the owner, Peter Nicholson, for use in the imposing Roman Catholic church then being built in Vernon River. This exhibition of Christian charity and brotherhood on the part of a neighbor outside the pale of his church was a source of great satisfaction to the worthy parish priest, Father James Phalen.

At the noon hour the mill-stream was the favorite resort of the Uigg school children. There they tied, on overhanging root or branch, the well-filled flask of precious milk, and, freed at noon, to it they rushed with headlong speed. The quick lunch over, along the banks they wandered, in and out among the drooping alders, eager searchers after hidden mysteries.

The mill-pond was stocked with excellent trout. In the mind of every Uigg schoolboy of the 80s and 90s is the picture of the six-foot-two figure of the patriarchal John Roderick MacLeod, brother of the noted lawyer, Malcolm MacLeod. Each day, about the end of the noon recess, his tall form might be seen approaching the school from the north, red beard floating in the breeze and long fishing rod over his broad shoulder, as he proceeded to his fishing post above the dam. On their way home from school, the children saw the mighty fisherman poised on his favorite stump, so far from shore that no one ever understood how he got there—smoking his pipe, and seeming to enjoy the quiet repose of that idyllic retreat.

In sharp contrast with this picture of rural ease was the scene often enacted a little farther down the road, as the school children passed the mill surmounted by its challenging weathervane.

There the genial owner, covered with flour, provoked beyond endurance by the patter of stones raining on the roof, was often compelled to rush from his work to drive off the mischievous school boys then competing to dethrone the saucy rooster that stood bravely defiant in the breeze.

This beautiful stream was at all times a favorite resort for those who loved the outdoor life, but particularly in summer time. The shady forest overhead, with here and there a spring of purest water issuing from the sandstone rock; the tipping sand piper, timorous crane, and occasional duck; the eager search under log or overhanging bank for the elusive and delectable sea trout, which at spring tides never failed to come, all added a charm and fascination to life that lifted the ardent dreams of youth from doubtful speculation to satisfied reality.

While wandering with rod and gun along this stream many a lesson was learned in hunting and fishing from a parent skilled in both.

Later, along these same haunting banks a youthful attraction ripened into unbroken friendship with those two genial and unfailing friends, John G. and William Matheson Macphail, whom The Ettrick Shepherd might well have had in mind when he wrote:

Where the pools are bright and deep,
Where the grey trout lies asleep,
Up the river and o'er the lea,
That's the way for Billy and me.

Where the blackbird sings the latest,
Where the hawthorn blooms the sweetest,
Where the nestlings chirp and flee,
That's the way for Billy and me.

Where the mowers mow the cleanest,
Where the hay lies thick and greenest,
There to track the homeward bee,
That's the way for Billy and me.

Where the hazel bank is steepest,
Where the shadows fall the deepest,
Where the clustering nuts fall free,
That's the way for Billy and me.

Each season had its own peculiar diversion for the young schoolboy. Fall and winter being the hunting season for fur bearing animals, the play of human wit against animal cunning added great zest to those dark and dreary days. The Orwell River always harbored a few mink. The simple box trap, baited with a freshly caught trout, first dragged along the ground to the trap, led many unwary animals to their doom. Their pelts generally sold for three dollars each, and, where tastes were simple and wants few, the prize was sufficient to give each member of the household a little token of the youthful hunter's affection.

Usually at least a dozen trips were made for each time the trap was sprung. When so found there instantly arose before the eye the image of a pelt, of size so great, and sheen so rare, that already in schoolboy fancy much of the fantastic price realized was spent in additions to the indulgent mother's and beloved sister's all too meagre wardrobe. But sometimes the quickly formed dreams of youth came to an equally sudden end. From the momentary, if high, pedestal of delight, the fall was crushing when, on cautiously peering through the partly opened door, there was descried two glistening terror-stricken eyes. What could it be? Surely no mink had eyes like these. With trembling hand the door was opened wider yet. Then, and not till then, did the friendly meow issuing from the dark recesses of that evil house dispel all fear, and reveal a marauding neighbor cat. The disappointment was only surpassed when, on a subsequent occasion, the same animal was convicted of a similar, but final, offence.

The joy at capturing a mink was measured to a certain extent by the price received for its pelt. In the case of the captured fox it was different. The thrill experienced by one who for days and weeks

has matched his wit, and won, against the craft
and cunning of the red fox cannot be imagined.
The woods at the back of the old farm extended
for several miles in an unbroken crescent from
Orwell North to Uigg and Dundee. This stretch
of heavy woods harbored many of the most cunning members of the fox family. They preyed on
the neighbors' poultry and were outlawed by
everyone. Those who were not interested in the
chase looked upon those who captured them as
public benefactors. Fox pelts, if taken in season,
were generally sold for about five dollars each.
On one occasion an eager hunter was following
hard on one of these raiders when the track led
into a hollow tree lying on the ground. Immediately blocking one end of the log with his coat, he
filled the other end with snow. Cutting a hole in
the centre Reynard was soon a prisoner. Nor was
the joy confined to the human family. There was
much competition for the privilege of gun bearer
on these expeditions. The moment the chosen one
sprang on the table to reach the old gun, Husk
was seen to tremble and his sleepy eyes to open.
When the outstretched arm had seized the gun his
quivering form and frenzied bark argued trouble
for the nimble red squirrel and fleet rabbit, game
in which the woods abounded.

The Nicholson home was a noted stop-
ping place. The genial host and hostess made

everyone welcome. Among those who frequently slept under its hospitable roof was George Munro Grant, later the illustrious Principal of Queen's University, then a missionary in Alberry Plains and adjoining districts. Angus A. MacLean, K.C., ex-M.P., of Charlottetown, recently told of how as a little boy he used to see Peter Nicholson, elder, in his pew in church every Sunday, rain or shine. Six miles of miserable roads had no terrors for these early churchmen. He recalls also that Mr. Edward Robinson, of Newtown, came to church with the first wagon (as the buggy was then called) in the district. Peter Nicholson had the second. Up to that time people either walked, or drove in carts or gigs. After the introduction of this new type of vehicle few, if any, had the moral courage to use the farm dump cart or two-wheeled truck on Sunday. Their proud Highland nature would not admit poverty, and rather than have their possessions seem mean by comparison they walked.

Beloved by all for his genial good nature, Peter Nicholson left this charming estate of 250 acres to his widow, Marion Munro, and three daughters. Marching for over a mile along both banks of the river from the Murray Harbor road westerly towards the sea, this tract of land was then, as it is today, a spot unsurpassed for quiet natural beauty. A few years ago it was purchased by Sir Andrew

Macphail, who, using it as a summer retreat, indulges his poetic fancy along its shady banks in pursuit of the delectable sea trout for which, from time immemorial, it has ever been famed.

La Grande Ascension was the name of the abandoned French settlement of about eighteen families, near the mouth of Orwell river. The Scottish settlers corrupted this into Sentie or Sengie. On the point was a shipyard owned by Benjamin Davies of Charlottetown, a Welsh shipowner, who there built many barques, brigs and smaller craft. Around this shipyard, as a boy, played his son Louis, who later, as Sir Louis Henry Davies, was for many years Chief Justice of Canada. He was born in 1845. His interest in the scenes of his boyhood escapades never abated, and a few years before his death in 1924, on his annual summer visit to Orwell, which he had not missed in forty years, he recalled with great amusement an occasion when his brother, in a fit of youthful rage, foiled in his attempt to catch him, threw a hatchet at his head. Had the missile found its mark Canada might have lost the services of a gentleman who, throughout his whole career, gave the best efforts of which he was capable to the public service of his country. He was always distinguished for his gracious manner, polished speech, and loyalty to friendships. These qualities contributed greatly to advance his career.

Farther up the river at the mouth of Currie's Creek as late as the early sixties John MacQueen and Donald Shaw built a schooner, and within the memory of several now living Donald "Stone-house" MacLeod, of Orwell, launched several schooners and brigs on the shore of the Stewart farm at Orwell bridge, where schoolboys now wade across the stream. These ships were built for sale. Many of them were loaded with the famed black oats or with potatoes, and sold with their cargoes to English and American investors.

Since those days the rivers have diminished in volume. The snows which formerly lay deep in the woods fed the streams for months, whereas today it is carried off by warm winds in a few hours, sweeping away bridges and mill dams in its mad course to the open sea.

Orwell School

The first school in the Orwell district was built of logs about 1825. It stood on the south side of the river, a few hundred yards below the site of the present bridge.

The first teacher in it may have been Samuel Martin, from Orwell Cove, or Donald Graham. The teacher boarded for a week at a time in each family, going through the settlement in this way. In 1839 or 1840 it is known that William

Ross, from Pictou, N.S., was teaching in the log school on Murdoch McLeod's farm, a little west of Orwell cross-roads. This school site was later abandoned for the present site of the church at Orwell cross-roads. This was about 1850. The first teacher in the school at this location was Alexander Maclean, who was born in 1831, and had attended the old log school while living with his sister Catherine, wife of John McQueen, in Orwell North. He was later graduated in Medicine from McGill University, and practiced in Montague. The second teacher in this school was probably Allan McDougall.

After a few years this building was moved to a point in Orwell North, on the farm later owned by Alexander MacKinnon.

The first teacher in this location was John Brooks from Murray Harbor, who taught in the years 1855 and 1856. The next building was of frame construction, on the same site.

When the boundaries of the Vernon River and Orwell districts were rearranged, the school site was again changed back to Orwell cross-roads, and here in 1895 a new one-room frame building was erected where it now stands, on the south-east corner opposite the Orwell church, where an earlier one had been built half a century before.

About 1850, when some of the oldest residents now living in the district attended school, the subjects taught were, Reading in English, Arithmetic, Geography, Spelling and Writing. No instruction was given in History.

When Mrs. Alexander Gillis, now living at Kinross, went to the Back Settlement (Lyndale) school about seventy years ago the master was Ewen Lamont, a worthy member of a talented family. The above subjects were the only ones taught then. The master lined the copy books in Gaelic, and also in an English translation of the Gaelic.

Each morning the New Testament was read, and one short period each week was spent on the Shorter Catechism, and on the rudiments of singing.

Mrs. Norman Samuel MacLeod of Uigg, now ninety-two years of age, recalls that in her youth the New Testament was the Reader used in the school she attended.

Founding of Churches
At Orwell and Murray Harbour Road

The population of Orwell had increased so much that the Presbyterians in that district decided to build a church at Orwell cross-roads on land donated to them by Peter Nicholson. Accordingly, in 1861, they erected the frame building which stands today. It was forty feet long by twenty-six feet wide, plastered throughout. The tower was ten and one-half feet square. It was surmounted by a low spire, on which stood a weather vane, unadorned by crowing cock. The parishioners supplied all the material, and most of the labor, free. In August, 1891, a frame structure twenty by forty feet was added. One-third the cost was paid by that good citizen, Alexander MacLeod, commonly called the Old Captain. The builder was Donald Martin of Uigg, brother of Martin Martin, Grandview, who built the first church.

For the first few years after the church was built, until permanent seats were installed, the congregation sat on planks placed for seats. Whatever these planks may have been they could not be more uncomfortable than the narrow straight-backed seats that were substituted for them. But this was not all. The painter, whoever he was, so mixed his materials that the worshippers stuck fast to the seat. Especially embarrassing was it for the ladies, who never knew whether their more delicate apparel would remain on themselves or adhere to the seat.

Margaret Neil MacLeod recalls, but cannot say that it was at the formal opening of the church, that the minister, Rev. Alexander Maclean, called on her brother James to lead the singing. He demurred. Mr. Maclean urged him, saying "It will be easier next time." The pastor's importunity prevailed and Mr. MacLeod led, and for some time thereafter was "precentor" in that church.

The writer recalls a few occasions in youth, watching with admiring eye, this same gentleman (then an aged man) feeling for the note, when yielding to the call of necessity he filled the absent precentor's place. If, late in life, Mr. MacLeod opposed the introduction of an organ into the same church, it was with the same gentle urbanity that ever characterized his life and marked him as one of nature's gentlemen. Beloved by all who knew him Mr. MacLeod passed to his reward two or three years ago, at ninety-two years of age.

The Orwell church was known to some as "Findlay's" church. Robert Findlay preached there occasionally. The Belfast minister used to conduct services in the church on every third Sunday. The Church Minute Book of 1872 occasionally mentions "Sermon read today." Mr. Findlay, on the occasions referred to, read a sermon and expounded the Scripture, sometimes to the amusement of the bashful, if irreverent, youths who clung to the back seats near the door, where they might not be denied the soporific pleasure of their favorite nicotine.

In the Minute Book of the congregation for 1872 Hugh Findlay is described as secretary of the Orwell section of the Belfast congregation.

The list of ratepayers with amounts agreed to be

paid is set out. The first half dozen are as follows:

Peter Nicholson £1 0 0
Capt. A. McLeod 12s 6
Mal. & John McQueen 6s 3
John McLeod (Sentie) 7s 6
John McQueen 12s 6
Angus McQueen 12s 6

The first interment in the Orwell churchyard was that of Dr. Archibald McLeod, son of the Old Captain, in October, 1884.

A few years subsequent to 1829 the followers of Rev. Donald McDonald erected a log church at Murray Harbor Road, now known as Orwell Head. About 1840 or 1842 this building was replaced on the same site by a large frame structure, plastered within. There was no tower. It was later found inadequate to accommodate the vast throngs that gathered there to hear their beloved pastor, so the building was sold to Duncan McDonald, son of Findlay, the minister's brother, who lived and died, unmarried, on the farm beside the church, formerly occupied by Murdo McKenzie, the schoolmaster. The said building is now used as a barn on said farm.

In or about 1864 the present imposing, but inartistic, frame church, was erected where the last one stood. It is sixty-two feet long by forty-two feet wide, with tall tower and taller spire, which was built on the ground and hoisted to position on the tower. There is a gallery at both ends and at one side.

Although a few members remained out, this congregation was received into the Presbyterian Church in Canada on July 7, 1886.

The minister's stipend for the first year was $600.00.

At the annual meeting held on December 12th, 1891, it was decided to buy an organ. This was installed in the church in the following spring, but not without opposition. At this time John S. Martin, later Speaker of the local legislature, was official precentor.

At the annual meeting held on December 12th, 1892, a letter was read from a member asking the meeting to vote the Presbyterian Hymnal into the church, but so great was the opposition that a vote was not taken. A year or two later it was introduced without opposition.

In June, 1928, the Orwell section of the congregation united with the Methodist churches at Vernon River and Cherry Valley, and the Orwell Head section united with the Valleyfield congregation, both in the United Church of Canada.

The following is a list of ministers of the Orwell Congregation:

Donald Ban McLeod (M.A. Park, Mo.; Lane
Theo. Sem.), July 28, 1887, to April 11, 1899.

Alexander J. MacNeill (B.A. Queen's),
November 21, 1899, to January 27, 1906;
born in Whycogamah, Cape Breton.

H. M. Michael (Glas. Univ.), December
23, 1906, to September 15, 1907; born
in Scotland.

Donald Ban McLeod (M.A. Park; Lane), June
20, 1908 to November 2, 1913.

W. H. MacEwen (Dal. B.A. Omaha Univ.;
D.D. Buena Vista, Iowa), October 1, 1914,
to March 25, 1923. Born in St. Peters, P.E.I.

G. A. Grant (M.A. Dal.; B.D. Pine Hill), April
2, 1924, to June 1, 1928; born in Pictou Co.,
N.S.

Henry Pierce (B.A. Mt. Allison), October,
1928; born in Winsloe, P.E.I.

Donald Macdonald, Thomas Boston Munro,
Malcolm MacLeod, and their respective families,
left Murray Harbor Road in 1874, and settled in
Schuyler, Kansas. Here they took up land and
became valuable citizens in inculcating a respect
for law and order, and in exercising a restraining
influence on the turbulent spirit then dominating the opening of that State. Among the flood
of immigrants then pouring into Nebraska, they
played an honorable part, and many churches and

schools in that state are living monuments to the unselfish labor, timely interest, and zeal of the two well educated Skyemen, Donald MacDonald and Thomas Boston Munro, and of their respective wives and families.

One of the nine sons of said Malcolm MacLeod was Donald Ban, who later returned to Orwell and was minister of united Orwell and Orwell Head congregation from 1887 to 1899.

He was graduated M.A. from Park College, Missouri, in 1881, and in 1883 from Lane Theological Seminary, Cincinnati, first honor man of his class. The same year he married Miss Stella Dyer, of Columbia, Missouri, a charming Southern lady. Their daughter, Elizabeth, is wife of Rev. William C. Wauchope, now of Buford, Georgia.

His first charge was at Nortonville, Kansas. From there he moved to Water Street Presbyterian church, Quincy, Massachusetts, and while there in 1886 his devoted and much beloved wife died. From 1887 to 1899 he was minister of the Orwell congregation: from 1899 to 1903 of Zion church, Charlottetown; from 1903 to 1908 of Union Square church, Somerville, Massachusetts, and again from 1908 to 1913 minister in Orwell. From 1913 to 1915 he was back in Quincy, Massachusetts, and from 1915 to 1918 he was pastor of his last charge (Upper Stewiacke, Nova Scotia) when failing health compelled him to retire from active work.

He started for Orwell, the place he loved so well, but his strength declined so rapidly that he was unable to continue the journey, and on May 23, 1918, while in Charlottetown, he passed away before he could reach the beloved district where he spent so many years of unselfish and devoted labor. Few clergymen have held the affection and esteem of their congregation in as high degree as did Mr. MacLeod. His influence on the youth of the community for a generation was profound. Urbane and cultured, he was at all times the most agreeable of companions. To Youth he was a companion, to Age a mentor. A man of broad tolerance, not too censorious of human frailties, he was not of that narrow and all too common class of churchmen who "attack prevailing fashions without any sense of proportion, treating follies on the same footing as scandalous vices."

A bronze tablet on the wall of the Orwell church, records the death in the Great War of the following members of the community:

1. Pte. Angus MacLeod, Winnipeg Mounted Rifles, born Feb. 20, 1875, died Sept. 15, 1916.
2. Lieut. Angus Nicholson, 16th Canadian Scottish, born Feb. 13, 1895, died March 5, 1918.

3. Sergt. Harold MacPhee, 105th Battalion,
born April 5, 1895, died Sept. 29, 1918.
4. Pte. John MacLeod, 20th Engineers U.S.A.,
born Aug. 1, 1894, died Nov. 9, 1918.

The following Gaelic message from Rev. John
MacLeod, a Scottish minister, was carried to the
elders at Orwell by Annabella, widow of Dr.
James Munro of Kilmuir, Skye, in 1840:

A few lines to the church.

*Tha Iain MacLeoid bhur brathair agus bhur
cosheirbhaisach anns an tighearn, a cur beanachd
a chum na seanair agus na'm braithrean dilis ann
a'n Griosda ann a'm Braith Orwell, agus a dh'ionn-
suidh nan uille thaag aideachadh ainm Iosa a guidhe
gu durachdach aig caihear na'n Ghras, gu'm biodh
an t-iomlan dhin air bhur gleidhadh gu tearuinte
trid air turai Tre an t-shoaghal thrioblaideach so.*

*Oir ged nach h-urrain sibhse mo ghuth a chlu-
inntean tha Neach eile ann a tha cluinntean ar 'n
uirnuighean uille.*

*Air an Aohbar sin that miag' iaridh bhur 'n uir-
nuighean air bhur sonninne anns an site so.*

You will present this among the Elders.

A few lines to the church.

John MacLeod, your Brother and co-worker in the Lord, sends a blessing to the Elders and the Faithful Brethren in Christ in the Parish of Orwell, and to all who acknowledge the name of Jesus, and earnestly prays at the throne of Grace that all of us be kept safely during our journey through this troublesome world.

Though it is not possible for you to hear my voice there is Another who hears all our prayers, and for that reason I beseech your prayers for us who are living in this place.

You will present this among the Elders.

Margaret McLeod, daughter of Neil McLeod, of Orwell Bridge, when recently interviewed in Orwell, spoke with eager interest of the early history of the settlement. Peggy Neil, as she is familiarly and affectionately known to the whole countryside, is possessed of a keen eye and a memory that would mark one with distinction at any age in life. Eighty-seven years spent wholly within the confines of her native Orwell have made her mind a repository from which those seeking to unravel the devious intricacies of family relationships, and local history, may dip but never sound the depths. The minutest details of the public and private life of the people are at her finger tips to give or withhold according as her wise discretion or fancy dictates. No one could be more willing to give than she, of this valuable store of knowledge, to those whose interest or pleasure it is to hand down to future generations an accurate record of the community as it was seen and understood by her.

"I recall," said Miss MacLeod, when recently seen at her home, "many of the original settlers. A more honest, upright, God-fearing people it would be hard to find. They all conversed in Gaelic, but most of even the original settlers later acquired English as well.

"Although times were hard our wants were few and simple, and I do not recall that we had to deny ourselves more than we do today. It may be that not knowing luxuries we never craved them. The only pleasures women engaged in were the 'ceilidhs,' which I suppose correspond to the modern 'teas.' The neighboring men and women gathered at each others' homes. The Highlanders were all fond of singing and music. The flute, fiddle and mouth organ were the usual musical instruments. There was always someone with an ear for music. At these 'ceilidhs' tales of witches and ghosts were told so vividly that we were often afraid to go home in the dark. Many of the women used snuff and some smoked the pipe. People were hospitable and one could always count on a warm welcome in every home. The church was the great meeting place, where old friends saw each other on Sunday. In spite of all the comforts of the present age I do not look back on the period of my youth as a too severe one, even if women did work more in the the open field than they do today."

Few, if any, of the old timers now living in Orwell have minds so stored with the history of past events in Belfast as Margaret Macqueen, who is now approaching eighty-four years of age. Her mother was a notable woman in her day. Born in Uig, Skye, in 1819, she emigrated to Prince Edward Island in 1829. At Montague River, in 1839, she married John Macqueen of Orwell. At that time the roads were simply a "blaze" through the forest. It was regarded as no hardship that the eight or nine mile drive from Montague River to their new home in Orwell North was made on horseback, bride and groom riding on the back of the same animal. This delightful old lady lived to be almost ninety-six years of age, passing away in 1915, with faculties unimpaired to the end. Though she was almost a centenarian she never conversed except in Gaelic. But in Belfast this was not unusual. In 1915 she was sprightly, cheerful, and fond of life; her kindly, lovable nature bursting forth in her favorite expression "Oh, *mo ghaol, mo ghaol*" (my dear).

"But," said Miss Macqueen, when recently talking about these events, "this drive was not considered any hardship. I recall myself as a young girl walking to Charlottetown and back the same day. This journey meant going up to the Head of Vernon River, for there was then no bridge at what was later called Vernon River Bridge. Many neighboring women did likewise. Among them I recall two of the most remarkable ladies whom I ever met. Rachel Gordon of Uigg, wife of John MacLeod, who lived to be almost ninety-eight, was one. The other was Miss Gunn from Miramichi, wife of his brother, Big Murdoch MacLeod. She lived for a century, all but three months, and up to her death a few years ago enjoyed perfect health. She thought nothing of starting on foot to Charlottetown, even at middle age, with shopping basket over her arm. She always completed the forty mile trip the same day in time to prepare the evening meal for her family.

"On these journeys along the Town Road we frequently met the New Perth and other settlers living along that road. They used a mode of conveyance that we never saw in use elsewhere. They called it a 'sliding car.' This device was made of two poles fastened to the hames with the rear ends on the ground. Across these poles were fastened boards, on which the kindly father carried over the weary twenty mile trail from town, to his anxiously waiting family, the meagre supply of provisions necessary to meet the simple demands of the frugal lives they lived.

"In our district, in those early days, produce was generally carried in huge home made linen sacks thrown across the horse's back. Grain was often taken in open row boats to Acorn's grist mill near Pownal. We often cut our grain at night. Young men and women gathered in crowds and worked with reaping hooks in the small fields surrounded by woods. Lit up by flaming birchbark torches on the end of long poles, the scene was an animating one. Many of the settlers made notable cheese. They cured it in grain stacks. This treatment gave a distinctive flavor greatly relished by those who partook of it.

"Although times were hard there were but few beggars. As there were no public institutions for the weak-minded, they wandered about the country, a constant source of anxiety to others. Everyone was busy. There was no reason or excuse for idleness when even the women and children could be usefully employed gathering slash from the cut-over land, when seasonal work failed. Only the wilfully idle had an easy time.

"Social conventions assumed a more important

part in the life of the district as wealth increased. When the famous Highland minister, Roderick MacLeod (known as Maighstir Ruairidh), then visiting at the Nicholson home in Orwell, came down to breakfast in bare feet, the daughters of the house were so surprised at the strange sight that they ever recalled it with amusement.

"The early settlers had few holidays. Christmas passed unnoticed. New Year's Day was the great day of the year. On the Eve of that day 'striking parties,' composed of young folk of the district, armed with sticks, marched through the settlement. When they arrived at a house they surrounded it, and to the accompaniment of music from the sticks beating the log walls, vigorously sang a Gaelic refrain, which may be translated:

> Get up auld wife, and shake your feathers,
> Dinna think that we are beggars,
> We're jist bairns come oot to play,
> Get up and gie us oor hogmanay.

"If, as happened but rarely, there was no 'Scotch' on hand, they were given cakes. But these were poor substitutes for what they sought, and the eager haste with which they directed their fleet footsteps to the light beckoning from the nearest neighbors' window, revealed an intention to ignore substitutes, and an anxiety to slake their inherited thirst by the only means known to them and to their forefathers for generations. When the log houses were replaced by shingled ones, these parties were discouraged and finally abandoned.

"There was no market for farm produce. The result was that laborers were paid paltry wages, as the following entry in an old Minute Book will show: 'Dec. 20/61. Norman McPherson began working with John McQueen for three years to serve at rate £2 for first year, £2 4s. for second year and £4 for third, and if proves well gets £6 for third year.'

"We were as content with our lot then as we are today. We denied ourselves what we knew we could not afford. This was an excellent training, and did much to build in the poor but proud Highlander a character marked by integrity and honor, virtues that he prized above life itself."

Founding of Uigg and Murray Harbour Road

Argosy never sailed with more precious cargo than that discharged at Charlottetown on June 1st, 1829, from the good ship *Mary Kennedy*. There were eighty-four heads of families in the party. They settled along the Murray Harbor Road, and in the Back Settlement, later called Lyndale. Each family bought from fifty to one hundred acres of land. They named the Uigg district after their birthplace,

Uig, in Skye, famed for romantic beauty, and deriving its name from the Norwegians who held the Western Islands of Scotland for generations.

The road from Vernon River to Murray Harbor had been opened shortly before the Uigg settlers arrived. In that whole stretch of territory there were then only three residents. One of them was Murdoch Mackenzie, a native of Inverness, who arrived in Belfast in 1821, accompanied by his wife Mary Mackinnon, and his father John Mackenzie. In 1822 he took up the farm on which now stands the Orwell Head church. He died in 1885, aged 100, leaving several children surviving.

The 1829 settlers found him dwelling in a log cabin, in the heart of the forest, with only a small patch of clearing about him. If life was simple and the world's luxuries few Murdoch Mackenzie had a fine mind. He opened a school in his little log cabin, and there devoted himself to the improvement of the minds of the sons and daughters of his near neighbors, who sent their children to the kindly Scottish schoolmaster to receive at his hands the solid groundwork of a liberal education.

After the morning lessons were heard this excellent teacher allotted his pupils their daily tasks. It was then his habit, on occasions, to seek repose on a bench beside the wall. Here he lay until gnawing hunger announced to the children the near approach of noon. All work was then laid aside; a great tumult was created until finally the master's form was seen to move. Rubbing his weary eyes he arose, and walked outside. There he gave one fleeting glance at the declining sun and returned to announce recess.

Later, when the country was settled farther south, Mr. Mackenzie opened a school in the Grandview district. Here he taught for many years.

Among the pupils inspired by Mr. Mackenzie with a love for education was Donald MacLeod, son of Donald Ban Oig MacLeod, who lived next door to the master. At an early age he moved to Parkhill, Ontario. His daughter, Katelena, recently told of her father's practice, continued till old age, of taking a Greek or Latin Bible to church, and following the reading of the Book in those languages, both of which he had mastered.

Rev. Donald Macdonald said of this noble man, that he was the only person in the whole countryside who possessed a knowledge of Greek. One of his daughters married Alexander (Garf) Macpherson, of Lyndale, and their descendants still reside in the district.

Perhaps in the history of the migration of the race no more highminded and worthy people ever entered a new land than those who came out on the *Mary Kennedy*. Their heritage of piety persisted undiminished for several generations in their new home. Like their forebears they were rigid Calvinists. The atmosphere of the district, like that of all Scottish districts of that age, was rather sombre. A small group, the Macdonalds, MacLeods, Gordons, Munros and a few others, were Baptists, who, for conscience sake, had withdrawn from the Presbyterian Church. Among them was a man of outstanding personality. Rev. Samuel MacLeod was born at Uig, in the Isle of Skye in 1796, and died at Uigg, P.E.I., in 1881, where he was buried in the Baptist churchyard. Over the destinies of this church for many years he presided, with inspiration not only beneficial to those who heard his earnest message, but also with benefit to that much greater multitude, who, through the continuing power of precept, and example, are unconscious heirs of the atmosphere of truth and rectitude that has continued long years after its inspirer has left the scene of these, his earthly triumphs.

So far-reaching was the influence of this small Baptist group in Uigg, that neighbors of other denominations testify that throughout their lives they have held the Baptist Church in especial veneration and reverence owing to the irreproachable lives and blameless character of this small group in Uigg assembled about their kinsmen and beloved pastor, the Rev. Samuel MacLeod.

If a reason is sought for the great success and high position attained by so many poor

Highlanders, not only in their own country, but also in lands across the seas, particularly in India and in Canada, it may be found in their sound education, and in that poverty, which inured them, from youth, to self denial. Early in life individual effort was demanded, and the valuable lesson was soon learned that it matters little what is earned if all is spent. The man who practises self denial and sets apart a portion of his earnings to accumulate and work for him in fair weather and foul, is the man who, in the end, attains wealth with its attendant power, and better still, character.

The forming of definite habits of self discipline and control is the guiding star that moulds the character and directs it into definite channels of self respect, independence, and integrity. Rarely is a person, who follows this line of conduct, found committing an unworthy action. The Uigg settlers, in striking degree, exemplify the fundamental soundness of this theory of life.

Rev. Donald Gordon Macdonald, of Vancouver, recently spoke as follows: "I was born beside Rev. Samuel MacLeod. To say that he was a man of outstanding natural ability is no exaggeration. His learning and wisdom were profound; his character irreproachable; his influence widespread; his example wholesome and contagious. In all my experience of eighty-six years of life, I look back upon the character of Rev. Samuel MacLeod as one of the most potent and significant things I have met. In speaking of him less than justice would be done were I to refrain from paying, in my own declining years, a final tribute to the memory of a group—the small Uigg group—of MacLeods, Gordons and Macdonalds, who constituted in themselves perhaps the highest expressions of the human family that it has been my privilege to know. When one reflects on the disregard for the rights of others so common in many ranks of society, the record of the Uigg district does much to restore confidence in human nature. Perhaps in no other place has there been a more willingly admitted regard for the rights of others. They seemed to recognize the great truth at the basis of the whole social structure, that the law is a great man-made institution, not only giving to each certain rights and privileges, but also placing on each heavy duties and exacting from each serious obligations. The instinctive grasp of this truth by the British people gives them their respect for law and makes them as a nation, in this regard, unique in the annals of history."

Uigg Grammar School

"Again I revisit the hills where we sported,
The streams where we swam, and the fields
    where we fought;

The school where, loud warn'd by the bell,
   we resorted,
To pore o'er the precepts by pedagogues
   taught."

The first settlers in Uigg were as zealous for learning as for righteousness. Their descendants of the
next generation were notable for the same qualities. Their school became a marked one, and in all
Canada none of similar grade, has a finer record
for an equal period of time. Since 1878 this school
has had two classrooms, and until 1909 all teachers came from families residing in the district.
During all that time numbers of scholars graduated from it, took special training and taught in
various other schools throughout the province.

These teachers were conscientious young men
and women. Eager in their pursuit of knowledge,
they inspired those under them with their infectious enthusiasm for learning. They generally
taught for two or three years and then pursued
a course of higher study in universities in the
other provinces, in the U.S.A., and sometimes
in Europe.

Dissension in the school was unheard of.
Each family regarded the little academy as in
its own especial care, and whatever service was
required, if tending to add to its honor and success, was given freely with eager enthusiasm

and cheerfulness. The success of the neighbor's child was a personal success reflecting honor, not only on the school, but on each and every family belonging to it.

The sympathetic attitude of the ratepayer stimulated the teachers to do their best. They knew their efforts were appreciated, and there was thus a bond between teacher and pupil rarely found in any other public school.

The pupils were tidy, clean and intelligent. The district being entirely Highland all could speak Gaelic, but at first all could not speak English. A distinct Gaelic accent was inevitable, and men from Uigg, who have never spoken Gaelic, carry the accent through life.

There were two classes in the Principal's room. The lower of these studied text books on English history, arithmetic, reading and writing. After passing into the highest grade Latin, algebra, geometry, French and geography were added. There was a blackboard for each class, also an atlas. The pupils were given problems to do at home, especially sketches in geography and short essays on subjects read or expounded in class.

In the eighties Malcolm MacLeod, K.C., presented an organ to the school. For many years, until destroyed by irreverent mice that nested in it, the scholars received great profit from the half-hour weekly song service. Being exceedingly shy this service helped to develop a self assurance and confidence which was often lacking in the country bred child.

The Principal taught the more advanced pupils for half an hour after the usual time for closing. They studied Greek, trigonometry, advanced geometry, and other subjects. Every morning when school opened each pupil in the Principal's room read a verse from the New Testament. After roll-call the day's work began.

The first building was erected of logs about 1840, near the present Uigg railway station, but on the west side of the Murray Harbor Road, and on the north side of the brook.

The following reference is from an old newspaper in the possession of Hon. D. A. Mackinnon, K.C., Charlottetown:

A SHORT ACCOUNT OF A LOG SCHOOLHOUSE AT ORWELL OR UIGG

"The first school houses were little log huts without any floors except the native earth. For a chimney two logs standing upright in the middle of the room, about three feet apart, served as jambs between which the fire was built to warm the children all around. On the top of these perpendicular logs of about four feet in height, was constructed the cob and clay work, namely: a mixture of mud and ferns between sticks, with the ends of each crossing those of the other like the walls of a log house. This formed the funnel aperture to throw off the smoke. Around this primitive and odd fireplace marched the monarch of the birchen rod and sceptre, with as much dignity over his mud floor as ever did Commodore of a large fleet over his quarter deck."

This building was replaced about 1849 by a frame structure, which was larger than the average one room country school of the present day. It stood a few hundred feet south of the present Uigg railway station, but on the west side of the road.

William M. Macphail, of Portland, Oregon, has a clear recollection of the building. A retentive memory under any circumstances, there was imprinted on his mind an image of the building, doubly clear from the fact that, as a child, his first day in school was spent in it. This was the last day it was used as a schoolhouse. There, with awe, he was shown the aperture in the ceiling through which offending Youth was forced to climb, and, in the Stygian darkness of the low-roofed garret, atone in gloomy silence and alone for misdemeanors done below. The menacing forms of ravenous rats and hungry mice, eagerly gnawing the surplus scraps from pupil's ample meal, assumed vast proportions and dreadful form in the innocent mind of the terrified child. The prescribed period of atonement over, Guilt descended to the room below, there to meet and suffer an even more unendurable fate, the scornful merriment of inconsiderate Youth.

Captain Neil Murchison of San Rafael, California, who was for a short period an attendant at this school, recently related the following incident:

One of the most noted masters of this old academy had decided on a visit to Charlottetown. He arranged that the school should be conducted by one of the older pupils in attendance during his absence. Circumstances, however, rendered the contemplated trip unnecessary, but so great was his interest in, and love for those under his care, that he could not refrain from attendance at his post of duty.

Arriving at the old school before even the most ardent football enthusiast appeared, he secreted himself in the dark forbidding garret, undismayed by hungry host of cunning rats and timorous mice. There he remained in secret silence, his mind noting with matchless grasp the actions of the various pupils in whose welfare he had such profound paternal interest. Not until the noon hour came and all had disappeared did he withdraw from his retreat, undiscovered by those whose actions he had so critically appraised.

This, the second Uigg schoolhouse, was used for the purpose for which it was erected until 1878, when it was vacated. Shortly thereafter it was moved to Kinross corner, and there used as a store by the owner, John J. MacLeod. The upstairs was converted into a hall, and within its walls the youth of the neighborhood received instruction in the value of sobriety and the folly of intemperance. It was also used by Thomas Richards, the music master of Alberry Plains. Here, on winter evenings, he taught his classes the rudiments of the science of music. It was in a very real sense a modern community centre, and for many years the various lectures, concerts, socials, magic-lantern shows, and other forms of amusement held in it, brought much happiness to the youth of the district. It was later moved to the farm of Mr. MacLeod in Uigg, where it now stands.

In 1878 the school trustees of the district, with the wisdom characteristic of those who have held the office for generations, erected a new frame schoolhouse, twenty-four feet wide by forty-five feet long, divided into two classrooms below, and public hall above, which they built that summer. This well proportioned, comfortable building, between 1878 and the present day has been the home of an educational institution, of its kind unsurpassed in the annals of Canada.

This building was erected by Peter Martin of Newtown, on the front of James Campbell's farm, about three hundred yards north of the site of the old schoolhouse. Probably the most imposing country school in the province when erected, this structure is today, after the lapse of over fifty years, a modern building, suitable in every respect for the purpose for which it is used. Enshrined about it are memories dear to the hearts of those who received instruction within its walls; memories of the kind that hold its former pupils, wherever they may be, with bonds of the deepest affection.

In the hall above the school classrooms, were held a debating society and occasional social gatherings in the winter evenings. The political meetings held there from time to time were attended by the men within a radius of many miles. The simple honest audience was greatly impressed by the learning displayed by the various candidates, generally inconspicuous country lawyers. Their ready flow of vigorous language, punctuated by occasional sallies of wit, amused, even if it did not instruct the hearers.

Of the descendants of the Uigg colonists now living no one is so well equipped to connect the present with the past as Rev. Donald Gordon Macdonald, who was born in Uigg, February 1843. At

eighty-six years of age Mr. Macdonald's memory
is unimpaired. He preaches almost every Sunday
in various Baptist churches in and around Vancouver, where he now resides with his wife, Minnie
Jane Schurman, a member of a notable Canadian
family, the Schurmans of Bedeque, Prince Edward
Island. Her brother is Jacob Gould Schurman, at
present American Ambassador to Germany.

In recent conversation Mr. Macdonald recalled
some of the well known characters in the settlement during the time of his youth.

"While quite a young boy," he said, "I lived
with my brother, Malcolm, a merchant of Belfast
Cross, now Eldon. Here I was known as 'Little
Donald at the Cross.' While living there I was
well acquainted with the Belfast minister, Rev.
Alexander MacLean. He was an able preacher
and well-liked minister.

"While living in the community I attended the
small Baptist meeting house near 'the Cross,'
which was attended by the few Baptists in the
district. There was 'Big Rory' McLeod and family,
a few Frasers, Martins, and Macdonalds. The
latter family lived at Pinette, and were marked
in that there were four Johns in the family—the
father and three sons all bearing the same name.
To distinguish them they were known as John
the Baptist (the father), John Small, John Ban, and
John. John Ban became a Doctor of more than

average skill, and a preacher of more than average ability. At an early age he moved to the U.S.A.

"At this time my old neighbor in Uigg, Rev. Samuel McLeod, frequently preached in the Baptist church nearby. He traversed the six miles from Uigg on horseback seated on a saddle of plaited straw, made by himself. Passing a group of young boys one day they laughed in derision at his humble saddle. His only comment was 'you need not laugh at my saddle, boys; every cent of it is paid for.'

"Samuel McLeod, like the other immigrants who landed in Charlottetown on the *Mary Kennedy*, May 31, 1829, had adhered to the Presbyterian Church in Scotland. While engaged as a schoolmaster in Skye, for conscientious reasons, he had allied himself with the Baptists, and made a public confession of his faith by immersion. For this he was waited upon by the school trustees and asked to resign. Owning the chair on which he sat, he replied 'I am more independent than His Majesty, our King. If he is dethroned he must leave his throne behind, but I take mine with me.' With his chair upon his shoulder he joined the departing settlers, and in the new land exerted an influence for good over a whole countryside.

"The following incidents may help show the moral authority exercised by Mr. McLeod over those who came within his influence.

"Two Roman Catholics, one of them a neighbor of Mr. McLeod, were engaged in heated controversy. Finally the neighbor said to his opponent 'It is folly for you to deny it, for with my own ears I heard Samuel McLeod say so.' The Irish disputant said 'Begorra, if Samuel McLeod said so, I believe it.'

"On another occasion two serious minded young boys were discussing the Day of Judgment. One said to the other, 'Where would you like to be on the Day of Judgment?' 'Inside Samuel McLeod,' was the prompt reply.

"Like his neighbors this noble man worked with his hands, six days in the week, to clear the primeval forest and create a home for himself and his family. On the seventh day he preached to them the Gospel, and by counsel and advice strove to lighten their load and improve their lot in the land of their adoption.

"Another man whom I recall vividly was the talented Daniel McKinley from a district near Charlottetown, who, about 1853, taught for a few months in the Uigg school and preached in the Baptist church. He posessed much more than average ability. Overstudy broke his health, and thereafter his life was devoted to a study of the Bible almost to the exclusion of every other interest. He could read it in seven different languages. The question of believer's immersion for baptism, instead of infant sprinkling, became for him a subject of supreme importance. He preached it everywhere, but his favorite method was to attend the church services of other denominations and sit near the door in order to be first out. He took his stand outside and preached to the retiring congregation. To any question asked he was ready with a reply, frequently to the amusement of the assembled crowd.

"On one occasion he attended the Murray Harbor Road church on Sacramental Sunday. Rev. Donald Macdonald, the minister, was conducting the service. McKinley began preaching by the roadside, and drew away some of the congregation from the service. Two of the elders advised him to desist. When he continued they carried him away bodily. In his clear stentorian voice, heard above the voice of the minister, conducting the service, he cried aloud, 'I am more highly honored than my Blessed Master. He was carried on one ass; I am carried on two.'

"At the close of a meeting in Pownal, the pastor (I think his name was Berry) whose limb had been amputated in England, to break the force of McKinley's argument for complete immersion, said: 'You could not carry out your theory in my case, for my limb is in England, and I am here.' 'It is better,' said McKinley, 'for you to enter into life maimed than having two limbs to be cast into hell fire.' To this the pastor replied, 'The only immersion I find in the Bible is the immersion of swine. They ran down into the sea and were choked in the water.' McKinley replied, 'The swine themselves had more sense than you Methodists. They went into the water to get clear of the devil, but you won't.'

"On another occasion McKinley went to St. Peter's Anglican church, Charlottetown, then, as now, noted for its High Church practices. What he heard and saw so grated on his sensitive mind that he could not endure it to the close of the service. Taking hat in hand he started for the door. On reaching it he turned, and facing the officiating clergyman said in a loud voice, 'That's what I call the fag end of Popery.'

"On another occasion I had a serious talk with McKinley over this question of baptism. I suggested to him that he was putting too much emphasis upon it. I pointed out that baptism is not a condition of our salvation, but rather an evidence of it. We are baptized because we are saved, not in order to be saved. 'Yes,' said McKinley, 'but you must ask them to go farther than is necessary in order to get them to go far enough.' "

For generations the acknowledged leaders at the bar, and in medicine on P.E.I. came from Uigg. Thence also came Sir Andrew Macphail, great in scholarship, distinguished in letters. His grandsire, William Macphail (1802-1852) of Nairn, Scot., together with his wife, Mary Macpherson (1804-1888) of Kingussie, and family, emigrated to Prince Edward Island in 1833. Their gifted son William (1830-1905), and his wife, Catherine Smith (1834-1920), parents of Sir Andrew, had the unique distinction of having a family of ten children of whom five sons and two daughters were university graduates of unusually distinguished records. At an early age he possessed a mind stored with the richest treasures of Scottish history, and a character moulded in the definite and fixed standards of a nation in which character building was one of the chief preoccupations of the people. From the first he was a conspicuous man. His acute mind, terse and vigorous speech, marked him for preferment, and soon, as school inspector, by his zeal, eager enthusiasm, and unselfish devotion to the cause of education, he laid, not only the district in which he lived, but the whole province, under heavy obligation to him for the impetus given to that sacred cause. His success in inspiring those who came under his influence with a love of the higher and nobler things of life was great, and many men and women in later life have testified to the great debt they owe that remarkable man.

Rev. Donald MacDonald
The Macdonaldites

The majority of the Presbyterians who settled in Murray Harbor Road and in Uigg in 1829 became followers of Rev. Donald Macdonald. This extraordinary man was the son of Donald Macdonald and his wife, Christine Stewart. The father's Jacobite sympathies were strong enough to lead him to face the King's troops at Culloden. Later he settled in Perthshire.

In addition to Donald, there were among other issue, Robert, of Perth; Duncan, and Findlay, of Orwell.

Donald was graduated from Saint Andrews University in 1816, and was ordained the same year. He emigrated to Nova Scotia in 1824 and settled in Cape Breton Island. He came to Prince Edward Island in 1826.

His brother, Findlay, had emigrated to Prince Edward Island about 1825, and settled near Georgetown. In 1829, or early in 1830, Rev. Donald was invited to Murray Harbor Road to preach to the newly arrived settlers, and liking the locality induced his brother, Findlay, to move to the two hundred acre farm half a mile east of Orwell Bridge, on the road to Kinross. Rev. Donald died February 21st, 1867. Findlay was then eighty-six years of age.

Mr. Macdonald was preaching at Birch Hill, Lot 48, when John Martin, Donald MacIan Oig McLeod, Murdoch Mackenzie, and other settlers, heard of his ministry. They conferred together and decided to send Donald MacIan Oig and Murdoch Mackenzie to hear him preach. If they reported favorably a "call" was to be extended to him to organize a church in their district. These emissaries were captivated by the magnetism, fiery enthusiasm, and obvious sincerity of the man. A feature of his service with which they were unacquainted was the "works" or trancelike ecstasy, accompanied by gesticulation and shouts, which overcame many of the audience. Donald took it upon himself to give the neighbors who gathered in his house to hear the report of the delegates, a physical demonstration of what he had seen. Donald MacIan Oig was a tall man. The ceilings were low. The beams were knotty. His first leap brought him in violent contact with the timbers overhead. His wife rushed for bandages, but he had caught already the infection of a religion he never forsook, and forbade her, saying "This guilty head, let it bleed."

The new minister came and preached in the barn on Angus Martin's farm, later Peter Musick's. His magnetism was infectious. Soon a body of loyal followers gathered about him and the Murray Harbor Road church became the nerve centre—of a parish which extended from end to end of the Island. Some, like the Lamonts, came and settled in the district to be near their beloved leader. Rarely has any pastor ever had a more loyal and faithful congregation than that gathered around Rev. Donald Macdonald, and rarely has a congregation been ministered to by a more tireless, enthusiastic, and effective leader. While he lived, and for years after his death, it was the practice in this church for the men to sit on one side of the church, while the women sat by themselves on the other side. In the long journeys between his various preaching stations he endured discomfort and great hardship. He never failed a waiting congregation, although frequently beset by the violent buffetings of the tempestuous island winter. Bitter cold, driving snow, or lashing rain were only a challenge to his unquenchable zeal.

Mr. Macdonald believed in celibacy, and in this and other respects was able to, and did, practice what he preached. The advantage of this condition, to a man ministering to so widespread a congregation, was incalculable. No man subject to the various distractions of married life could possibly have accomplished what he undertook and did. Cut off, as he was, from the refining and mellowing influences of wife and family, he developed a reserved dignity of exterior while yet retaining a warm and tender heart within. When a member of his congregation started out with her crying child, he called after her, "Sit down woman, and teach your child obedience." The kindly gentle mother sank into the nearest pew overcome, but so well understood was the greatness of the man that no resentment was harbored by the one whom he had rebuked.

When Angus Joiner (McLeod), while yet a young man, became a convert of Mr. Macdonald, he was admonished by him to put aside the violin he loved to play "as belonging to the flesh." Angus took it out and destroyed it with an axe.

Every man was influenced by his environment and so was Mr. Macdonald. His place was with the afflicted and distressed, with the sick and the dying. He was not called where there was gaiety and merriment. He took on the atmosphere in which he lived, as do all men. But if he was not their intimate in joy, he was in that emotion that is even more universal—sorrow. Through this common bond he entered their inmost hearts and became the constant friend and confidant of all.

Whenever grief entered the home, the form of the beloved pastor followed close behind to chase away their sorrows, with the sunshine of an understanding sympathy, and a desire to serve that knew not labor.

Hence it was that when the body, broken in the

service of others, was carried to Orwell, to the home of his brother, Findlay, there to die, tears coursed down the furrowed cheeks of stern men, as they looked for the last time upon the austere face, guardian of the tender heart, that never failed them in the hour of their adversity and of their sorrow.

On the monument erected to his memory in the Orwell Head churchyard is the following inscription with a Gaelic translation:

In Memory of
Rev. Donald MacDonald
Minister of the Church of Scotland, who was born
January 1st, 1783, in the Parish of Logierack Perthshire, North Britain. Educated in the University
of St. Andrews, and ordained by the Presbytery of Abertaill in 1816.
He emigrated to America in 1824, and laboured
in his Master's cause on the Island for nearly forty
years, with many tokens of acceptance.
He died on the 22nd day of February, 1867, in the eighty-fourth year of his age, and the fiftieth of his ministry.

Rev. Mr. Macdonald was the first person interred in the Murray Harbor Road churchyard. James Campbell of Uigg was the first interred in the kirk cemetery on the front of Samuel Martin's farm, near the junction of the Dundee Road and the Murray Harbor Road.

One of the oldest women living today is Mary Munro, widow of Allan MacSwain of Lorne Valley. She was born at Shawbost, Parish of Lochs, Lewis, in 1834, and emigrated with her family to the Orwell district in 1842. Her twin sister Anne, died only two years ago. For a person of her age she possesses remarkable hearing and memory. Few people have had her variety of experience. Pioneering for almost a century, few now living know more of early days on the Island than she.

Quite recently several friends visited this gentle old lady at the home of her nephew, Daniel Mac-Swain, in Lorne Valley. Her interest in the things of every day life was a surprise to those who met her. Although it is almost ninety years since she left the land of her birth, with true Highland sentiment her mind returned to those early days of happy childhood in the glens of far off Lewis and Skye.

"Although born in Lewis," said she, "my father was a native of the Parish of Kilmuir, Skye. He was one of that noble band of Scottish schoolmasters and catechists, who held aloft the torch of learning and religion in their own and in foreign lands to such purpose that the name Scotland became synonymous with intelligence and honor the world over. For many years he taught and preached in Skye, but when I was born he was teaching in Lewis. The schoolmaster's wage was small, as is proved by various receipts signed by my father in a little Day Book, once owned by a Skye shopkeeper, but now possessed by my nephew, Dr. Alexander Allan Munro of New York.

'Received from Alexander Duncan, Esq., Treasurer to the Honorable Society in Scotland for propagating Christian Knowledge, the sum of seven pounds ten shillings sterling, being the amount of my salary from the first day of May to the first day of November last, as school-master at Fernlea, in this Parish, which sum I hereby discharge the said Treasurer.

'Witness my hand at Fernlea, Parish of Bracadale, this 29th day of January, eighteen hundred and twenty-two years.'

Sgd. ALEX MUNRO.

"For generations the Munros were preachers and teachers and many of them follow these vocations today.

"The first recollection I have, certainly the first that can be fixed definitely," continued Mrs. Mac-Swain, "was the death of King William IV. My father came into the room where we were sitting and spoke to mother. She raised her apron to her face and burst into tears. This was the first time I ever saw my dear mother cry, so I became alarmed and cried too. This started my twin sister. Mother then took us both in her arms and petted us. 'The king is dead,' she said, 'don't mind, everything is all right, we are going to have a little girl Queen.'

"I recall that everyone was talking America and how prosperous their friends there were. There seemed to be dissatisfaction and unrest. Times were hard and getting harder. Finally, after much anxious thought, my father decided to sever the age-long tie that bound us to the Hebrides, like oaks to the very ground. We packed up the few indispensable worldly goods and started for Prince Edward Island.

"I can yet see," she went on, "the coast of that land of promise looming up ahead of us as we approached its shores. After visiting relatives in Orwell and Alberry Plains, we took up land with other Gaelic speaking settlers in Brown's Creek. We were not long in our new homes before father, ever following the lure of education, helped to organize a school. A Free Church congregation was also soon established. The ardor of the people for it almost partook of hostility to the neighboring Established Church at Murray Harbor Road. The 'Disruption' had recently taken place in Scotland. The newly arrived immigrants were keen partisans, and bitter foes of the Establishment.

"But," said Mrs. MacSwain, "our Highland blood kept us moving and once again we broke up our home. With several neighbors we moved to the Head of Cardigan, then one of the most heavily wooded districts on the whole Island. No one can realize the toil involved in clearing the maples. The stumps never seemed to die. However, we stuck and this move proved our last. We liked to visit our old Brown's Creek neighbors, and we frequently drove across country on Saturday for the Sunday service, staying with friends over the weekend. Among the adherents of this congregation was William Lamont, the only member of that devoted church family not a follower of Reverend Donald Macdonald. Although not a gifted singer William Lamont was an expert 'liner.' This was an important part of the precentor's duty, and it was well performed by him. At a time when each person in the audience did not possess a book, it was necessary, if all were to sing, for someone at the beginning of each line or two to intone the words in a voice heard by the whole audience. This was known as 'lining.' Once done each person had the words, and was thereby enabled to raise his voice in song. All sang, and sang fervently, and if all did not pray, those who did appropriated the time that would have been taken up by others had all prayed. The result was hearty, refreshing singing, and long tedious prayers.

"On one of these occasions the Cardigan visitors were holding a service on Saturday evening at the home of one of their Brown's Creek friends. William Lamont was lining, and all present were entering with the greatest fervor into the song. It was fall, and Boreas smote the log walls of the humble cottage with bitter blasts. The household dog had been driven from his accustomed haunt beside the open hearth, to make way for the press of visitors. Towards the end of the first song, a dismal howling was set up by the faithful Achates without, his spirit moved as much by the mournful and unusual harmony within, as by the bitter blasts without. At length the song was ended. The last note had scarcely died away before the precentor, in the same wavering tone, and with the same fervid expression, carried on in Gaelic, 'Chaidh Satan a steach do'n choin' (Satan has entered into the dog). Thinking him still 'lining,' the congregation, swept along by the enthusiasm of the occasion, took up the refrain, and from every throat there arose, loud in unison, 'Chaidh Satan a steach do'n choin.' But if His Satanic Majesty had entered into the dog, as alleged by the respected precentor, his sojourn in the canine host was of short duration, for there was ample evidence in the frequent fistic encounters between the more quarrelsome members of the two rival religious factions, at casual meetings over the flowing bowl, that he soon freed himself from the restraints of his shaggy habitation, and invaded the more congenial soil of the human heart.

"What do I think of our young folk today?" said Mrs. MacSwain, repeating the question of one of her visitors. "Well, although I do not read many periodicals or newspapers, I do not agree with the criticism I sometimes hear and read of the character of the modern girl. After almost a century of association with my friends and neighbors I must say that human nature does not differ appreciably today from what it was when I was a child, or during any period since. The fact of the matter is, too much stress is laid today on formal education. I have met women in rude surroundings possessed of as much refinement of mind and gentility of manner as is found in those reared today in luxury. Youth makes its mistakes, no matter what the circumstances."

Mrs. MacSwain does not look like a person who ever endured great physical hardship. When one of her guests referred to the freshness of her complexion, her face lit up with animation.

"My continued good health," she said, "is due to the simplicity of our lives. We never indulged ourselves. Our surroundings were healthful and natural. We were taught to face the future with a fortitude that is not looked for in women of the present age. For women to give way to tears was considered unseemly. In my early years it seems to me that women were almost as strong physically as men. I have seen cases of harrowing misery caused by intemperance. The curtailed use of intoxicants has already done more to lighten the burdens of the poor than any single agency operating in the century of my existence."

Mrs. Norman MacLeod, of Vancouver, when discussing early Belfast shortly before her death about a year ago, told of herself and two sisters having received collegiate training. Her brother, Angus MacSwain, was graduated in arts and medicine from McGill, and Harvard, and later took post graduate courses in European universities. Other families had a similar record.

"Parents in those days," said Mrs. MacLeod, "were anxious to educate their daughters, but the times were hard, and it was difficult to pay for the education of more than one or two members of a family. At that early time the economic freedom of women had not been realized; it had not even been attempted. The only vocation in which she could hope to use a specialized training was school teaching. The few who received high school training became teachers."

Mrs. MacLeod was of the opinion that though the vast majority of the women of early Belfast went to the common country schools only, they were thoroughly grounded in the fundamentals of education. "The first lesson," said Mrs. MacLeod when questioned on that point, "impressed upon the mind of the young girl was never to strive to do or to think as men did or thought, but to do and to think in a way befitting the physical and mental character of those of their sex. It was considered quite enough if a girl was able to do well those things that more fittingly fell within their province. Women of past generations were not as cultivated as are modern women, but they were endowed with equal refinement. Their influence in the home was as potent as is that possessed by their modern sisters.

"In looking back," continued Mrs. MacLeod, "over the list of Belfast women, there comes to mind the names of many of great charm and refinement. Among them none made a more indelible impression on my mind than did Mrs. Donald A. MacLeod of Eldon, formerly Miss Ann MacKenzie, sister of Findlay MacKenzie[2],

---

2   Father of Dr. David V. MacKenzie, the eminent surgeon of Montreal.

and Captain Roderick MacKenzie of Flat River. Never in my life have I met a woman of higher culture and greater charity than that wonderful woman. About her there centered to the end, which came only a few years ago, when she was over ninety-one years of age, the distinguished and charming family of sons and daughters, who gathered each summer at the old home, attracted by one of the most beautiful characters it has ever been my privilege to know."

The Mackenzies of Belfast as a clan were noted for nobility of looks and character. Even among them Mrs. MacLeod was pre-eminent.

Another interesting old lady, full of the lore of old Belfast, is Jessie, daughter of William MacLeod, of the Glashvin, Pinette family of that name. Her father fought in the Napoleonic Wars, and from his own lips she heard many romantic tales of stirring scenes in foreign lands. Although eighty-nine years of age her memory and hearing are unimpaired.

William Saighdear, as he was commonly called by his Gaelic speaking neighbors in Uigg and Orwell, was a sergeant in the 42nd Highlanders — the famous Black Watch. He enlisted when sixteen years of age, and continued with the colors for twenty-one years, when he was honorably discharged with several medals and a pension. After returning from the wars he married Catherine

Macpherson. In 1831 the family emigrated to Uigg, P.E.I., and here in 1840 Jessie, the youngest and sole survivor of their ten children, was born. Her husband, Angus R. MacSwain, Lorne Valley, died a few years ago, and she now resides with her daughter, Christine A. Gurney. She is perhaps the only woman now living whose father fought at Corunna. She recently spoke of him as follows:

"He stood six feet three inches, and was a magnificent specimen of manhood. Skye gave many such men to the British Army. Their bravery did much to augment Britain's glory. He had many harrowing experiences in the Peninsular War, through which he fought under Sir John Moore and Wellington. On three occasions bullets were extracted from his body, and on one occasion he received a sabre wound in the shoulder. At Corunna he was left badly wounded on the field. An English officer and orderly came upon him. The orderly examined the wounded Highlander and told the officer that he was too far gone to do anything for him. On hearing this, father, turning to the orderly, said, 'If I had a bullet you would lie with me.' The brave and compassionate officer was so struck by the undaunted bearing of the man that he said, 'This is a brave man, we will take him.' So saying he dismounted and together they placed the disabled soldier on the horse. Coming to a house near which goats were

feeding, they asked a woman for milk for the suffering man, and a bandage for his wounds. She
immediately tore a strip from her chemise, and
with this his wound was bound. After recovering
he fought in many more of the bloodiest battles of
the War, receiving wounds but finally returning
to England.

"In Waterloo he was shot through the abdomen,
and thought his end had come. He recovered,
however, and returned to Skye. In Uigg and Head
of Cardigan, he underwent the many and varied
hardships of pioneer life without complaint.
Finally his powerful frame and masterful spirit
succumbed to the hardships he had undergone.
They carried him from Lorne Valley to the Belfast
churchyard, and there they left his remains among
the clansmen he had followed to their home in
the new land. His devoted wife, my ever kind
mother, rests by his side."

UIGG OF TODAY

For three generations after its settlement Uigg,
like Belfast, remained a remote, isolated district.
Untouched by the surging mass of humanity
that swarmed over the continent, its frugal and
industrious residents retained the customs and
beliefs of their forefathers to a degree rarely found

elsewhere. Those who never left its shores thought the little isle on which they lived the centre of all things, and those living beyond its shores were looked upon and referred to as foreigners. Their business was done with Boston, and that home of culture was better known by many of them than hamlets a few miles distant from their birthplace. It was in the U.S.A. that the surplus population sought and found employment, and there were few Belfast homes but had sons and daughters prosperous and loyal citizens of that great republic. The bond of sympathy for America was strong, and for years many hoped for political union with the States.

About twenty years ago, when the first train steamed into Uigg, the district awoke from its long sleep. It is no more a remote, out-of-the-way, isolated district. Trains, automobiles, telephone and telegraph have brought it into close touch with the outside world.

The entire population devotes itself to farming. Each homestead generally consists of one hundred acres. The dwelling houses are commodious and comfortable. Most of them are built of native spruce and fir, which is sawn in local mills. A few have hot-air furnaces, some of which burn hardwood from the little groves wisely preserved on almost every farm. The early settlers grew oats so persistently that the soil became greatly

impoverished. In late years it has been restored
to its former fertility through rotation of crops,
fertilizers, and raising of stock. For the past few
years large quantities of certified seed potatoes
have been grown. These are shipped to points as
far afield as Cuba, and the Carolinas. Co-opera-
tive marketing has superseded individual effort,
and now eggs, cattle, sheep, pigs, potatoes, and
all the products of the farm are handled through
the various pools organized for the purpose.

One of the most notable changes in Uigg is that
in the home. In the early days a family of ten children was not uncommon. There were several of
twelve and one of fifteen. Today a family of half
a dozen is rare. The effect on school and church
is depressing. The old enthusiasm is lacking and
there is a slackening in effort and attendance.

But nothing can rob Uigg of the glory of its
past, and there will cling to it always something far above material things. The memory
of its pious, law-abiding, God-fearing men and
women will long be cherished by such as love
nobility of character and upright conduct. The
high tradition of the founders has been in large
measure maintained by succeeding generations,
and now a century after the first settlers set up
their temple in the wilds of Uigg, their descendants may proudly claim that, in the century of
its existence, no resident of that much loved spot

has ever been charged before a court with the commission of a crime.

> "But if, through the course of the years which
> await me,
> Some new scene of pleasure should open
> to view,
> I will say, while with rapture the thought
> shall elate me,
> 'Oh! such were the days which my infancy
> knew!' "

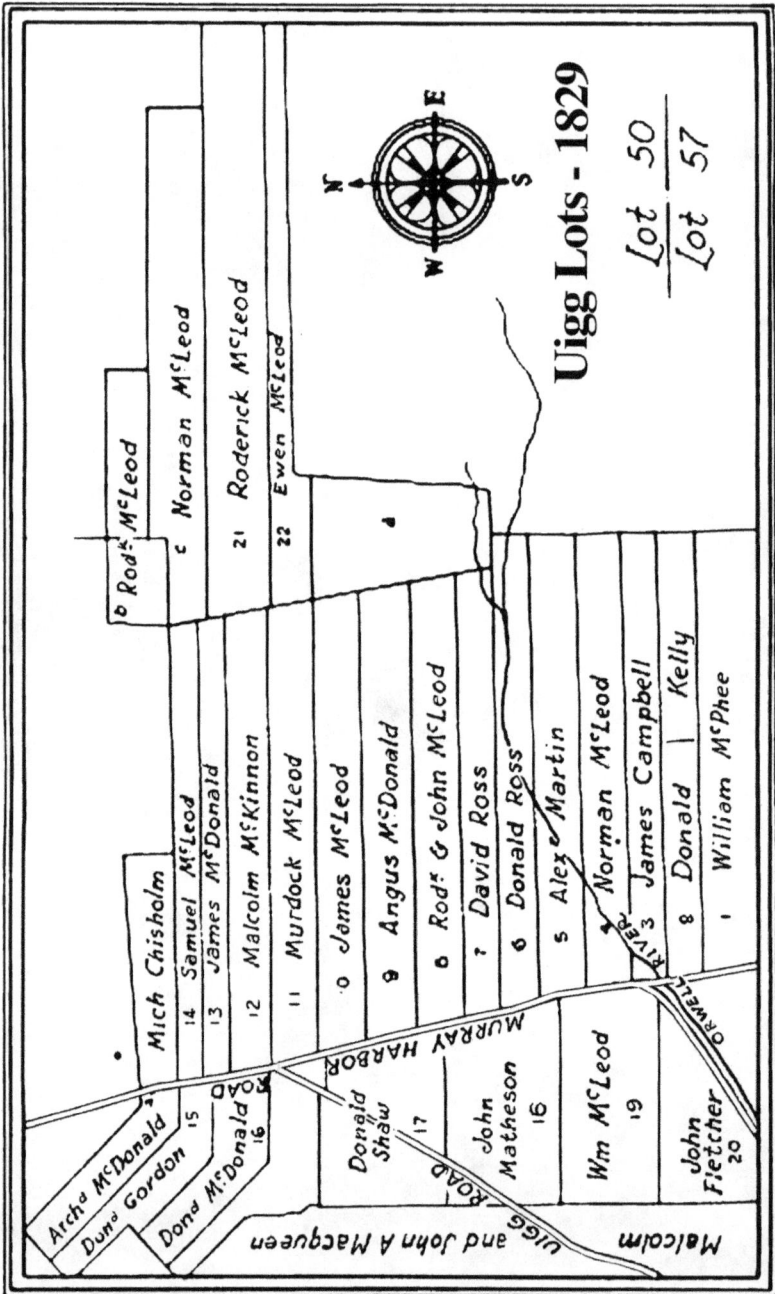

Uigg Lots - 1829

Lot 50
―――――
Lot 57

Part Two: Founding of Uigg

The Founding of Uigg

In a little Minute Book in the custody of Samuel MacLeod, Uigg, in the handwriting of Malcolm MacLeod, K.C., a native of Uigg, is the following brief authoritative history of the founding of that district.

Uigg in Queens County, Prince Edward Island, was settled in the year 1829 and 1831 by immigrants from the Isle of Skye, Scotland. The immigrants of 1829 were chiefly from Uig, in Skye, and in memory of the place of their birth, they called their new home in the woods of Prince Edward Island, Uigg. The first map in this book shows the original farms and the names of their first permanent occupants. Beginning on the eastern side of the Murray Harbor Road (which was made through this settlement in 1828) and on the south side of the settlement, there are William MacPhee, Donald Kelly, James Campbell (who had bought out one Allan McDonald, called Allan MhacHamish), Norman MacLeod and Alexander Martin; who had entered into possession of their farms in 1827, James Campbell, however, only going into

actual possession in 1829 as successor to Allan
MhacHamish. Donald Ross and David Ross
(whose father lived on the road crossing from
Orwell to the Murray Harbor Road) had taken
their farms but did not go into actual possession till a few years after 1829, probably 1833
or 1834. Roderick McLeod and John McLeod
(with their father, Norman McLeod), Angus
McDonald, James McLeod, Murdoch McLeod,
Malcolm McKinnon and James McDonald,
went into possession in 1829, the year in which
they arrived from Skye. A few years afterwards
the Rev. Samuel McLeod bought and entered
on the north half of James McDonald's farm.
Michael Chisholm, whose people were from
Strathglass, near Inverness, was several years
later in coming. To the westward of the Road
were Donald Gordon, Donald McDonald and
William McLeod (known as Ulliam Sceighdear),
who arrived from Skye in 1831. Donald Shaw
was born in Pinette on this Island, and he and
John Matheson (from Skye also) went on their
farms about 1833. The farm marked Fletcher
was originally occupied and before 1829, by one
Gay, from Lot 49, called by the Highland people
"Gaieach Cam," who built a saw mill. His son,
John Gay, afterwards occupied the farm and
sold it to John Fletcher, who built a grist mill
further up the stream (where John F. McLeod's

mills were) sometime about the year 1840 or 1845. The farm marked Archibald McDonald was taken by Archibald (son of James) some ten (10) years after the original settlement. Of the farms to the rear or eastward, the one marked Roderick McLeod was taken by him about 7 or 10 years later than 1829. His brother, Ewen McLeod, went into possession of his farm 2 or 3 years still later. Of the original occupants above named there are only Roderick McLeod and his brother John and David Ross, still living on the land of which they took the original possession. James McDonald and his wife (a sister of Roderick, John and Samuel) are still living, but removed from Uigg several years, and are now living with their daughter at Green Marsh, on Murray Harbor Road. Of the original settlers, Norman McLeod, James McLeod, and Murdoch McLeod, were an older generation, and were brothers. John McLeod, Roderick McLeod and the Rev. Samuel McLeod were also brothers, and sons of Norman, known as Tormoid 'ic Neal 'ic Murchuidh, Gillie Brighe, 'ic Murchuidh. Angus, James and Donald McDonald were also brothers.

In these days the whole face of the country was covered with a dense forest, and the first settlers, perfect strangers to the use of the axe on their arrival, had little but their labour to depend on for making a living and rearing and educating numerous families.

The first school house for the settlement was built about 1840, to the northward of the stream of the Orwell River, and to the west of the Murray Harbor Road, near the top of the ascent from the brook, in a dense spruce bush, a portion of William McLeod's woods. It was a long building, perhaps 20 × 15 or 18 feet, roofed with boards and slabs, having the spaces between the round logs filled with moss. The fireplace was open, having its sides or "jambs" of wood like inverted sleigh runers. The first teacher was one Donald Kelly (a relation of the Donald Kelly whose name appears on the map), who arrived from Skye in 1839 or 1840. He and his wife and one or two children lived in the school house for a year or two. Parents paid him one pound per annum of the then currency ($3.24) per pupil, and gave him besides, for his support, one bushel of wheat each family.

The Rev. Samuel McLeod was a Baptist minister and up to the time of his death officiated ministerially for the people with no stated stipend, with no pay whatever for many years, and indeed never required or expected anything. Any small help or offering made him was always reluctantly received. Of the families of the settlement shown on the first map, only Nos. 8, 9, 10, 11, 12, 13, 14, 15, 16, 17, 21 and 22, were stated worshippers at his services. The rest of his congregation were persons of his denomination from the adjacent country. At first the Sunday and weekly meetings were held in the dwelling houses of the farms above mentioned, and also in the McLeod's own house; the meeting being held in the houses on successive Sundays. In summer they placed temporary seats on their barn floors as being more roomy and cooler than their dwellings. The services were conducted in Gaelic and for Psalmody they used the version of the Gaelic Psalms authorized by the Church of Scotland. Mr. McLeod was a man of extensive information, sincere piety, good abilities as a preacher, an original thinker, and a man universally respected. All who knew him were his friends. Gradually his services became partly Gaelic and partly English, and for some years before his death, the services were conducted entirely in English. This became necessary owing to the deaths of the older people and the preference of the younger generation for English, and in some cases their ignorance of Gaelic, and the addition to the church of persons whose

mother tongue was English. About the year
1852, the people built a small wooden church on
the ground used as a burial ground, and from
that time the services in dwellings ceased. For
the first 15 or 20 years few changes took place
in the occupations of the farms, and although
deaths occurred occasionally, families, as a rule,
kept together, and the population of the settlement increased very fast. But after that time, the
young men first, later the young women, began
to go abroad, and the older generation yearly
died more rapidly, so that at this date there
is almost an entire change in the occupants of
the farms.

This map was copied by a surveyor (a
stranger) from a map a few years older than
this writing, and for correct use of it, it is necessary to state that the farms marked Samuel
McLeod 50ac. and Malcolm McLeod 50ac. now
are owned by Malcolm McLeod, son of Rev.
Samuel McLeod. Murdoch McLeod on that
map is not the original Murdoch McLeod, but
a son of the old Norman McLeod. The farm
marked Donald Ross is occupied by Donald
Martin, house-joiner. The farm marked Malcolm McLeod (formerly Angus McDonald),
though owned by Malcolm McLeod (Barrister), is actually occupied by his father, Roderick

McLeod, already mentioned as one of the original settlers.

A piece of ground indicated on the map, was from the first set aside for a burying ground. The first person buried there was Norman McLeod, the old man already mentioned, who died in the year 1837. No record of burial was kept. To supply that omission, this book was prepared. There are yet living persons who remember the first burial and can still identify every grave. From the information of such persons and from the families and friends of the deceased, the record of the earlier burials is made up. The dates in some cases have been taken from existing tombstones, from friends and relatives; in other cases, approximated; and in some cases cannot be got.

The above sketch indicates the changes in the last 52 years. Whoever lives and takes the trouble of noting the changes in the next fifty years will have to narrate still greater and more rapid changes, but he will not have to write about a more honest, industrious, or worthier people, than the first inhabitants of Uigg.

MALCOLM MCLEOD (Barrister)
Saturday, 27th Jan., 1883.

Copy of Clearing Paper
P.E.I. Register and Gazette, Tuesday, June 2,
1829

84 Immigrants including women and children from the Isle of Skye arrived here on Sunday. They left their native place about 6 weeks ago in a ship for Cape Breton along with a number of settlers for that Island. They seem all to be in high health and judging from appearance in easy circumstances.

With prudent foresight characteristic of their race they came provided with 12 months provisions and an ample stock of warm clothing. They have all relatives already settled in the Island chiefly about Belfast, and with the exception of one family it is, we understand, their intention also to locate in that thriving settlement.

Custom House, Entered June 1st, 1829.
Mary Kennedy, Cape Breton, 84 passengers.

Occupants of Farms

Original Occupants	1883 Occupants
1. William McPhee	Family left settlement: Mal. Campbell, son of No. 3
2. Donald Kelly	James Kelly (of part) his grandson
3. James Campbell	John Campbell, his son
4. Norman McLeod	John McLeod, his son
5. Alexander Martin	Jas. McKenzie, his son-in-law
6. Donald Ross	Family removed—Donald Martin
7. David Ross	Same
8. Roderick and John McLeod	John sold to Malcolm (Rodk's son) who still holds his
9. Angus McDonald	Family left—Farm owned by Malcolm McLeod, occupied by Roderick McLeod
10. James McLeod	John McLeod, his son
11. Murdoch McLeod	Family left—Norman Murdoch McLeod, son of Norman
12. Malcolm McKinnon	William McKinnon, his son

Occupants of Farms

Original Occupants	1883 Occupants
13. James McDonald (Family gone)	Malcolm McLeod, son of Rev. Samuel McLeod
14. Samuel McLeod (Died)	
15. Donald Gordon	Donald McQueen—no connection
16. Donald McLeod (Family left)	Ferris and John McLeod—no connection
17. Donald Shaw	Allan Shaw, his son
18. John Matheson (Family left)	Malcolm McKinnon—no connection
19. William McLeod (Family left)	Alexander MacLeod. (His widow, Elizabeth Susan MacLeod, the well known writer and poetess, resides in Charlottetown with her sons Victor and Stanhope.)
20. John Fletcher (Family left)	William McPhail and J. F. McLeod
21. Roderick McLeod	Murdoch E. and John S. McLeod, his sons
22. Ewen McLeod	Malcolm McLeod (son of Roderick)

Occupants of Farms

Original Occupants	1883 Occupants
24. Michael Chisholm	Mrs. Chisholm, his widow — Neil McPherson

(a) Archibald MacDonald		Same
(b) Roderick McLeod	Recent	His Family
(c) Norman McLeod	Occupation	Same
(d) Ewen McLeod	Comparatively	John Roderick McLeod

Uigg, P.E. Island
Saturday, 27th January, 1883

Occupants of Farms
in 1929

1.   Hugh Martin, son-in-law of John Campbell.

2.   Samuel Campbell, son of John.

3.   Simon Donald Campbell, son of John.

4.   Samuel Hume, son-in-law of Donald Campbell.

5 & 6.   Adrian Reynolds, married Euphemia Macpherson, Granddaughter of Malcolm Campbell.

7.   John A. MacLeod, son of John F. MacLeod, miller.

8.   John J. MacLeod, brother of Rev. D. B. MacLeod.

9.   John W. MacLeod, grandson of William Taylor MacLeod, Dundee.

10 & 11. John MacLeod, son of Murdoch.

12.   William Mackinnon, son of Charles.

13 & 14. Samuel MacLeod, son of Malcolm.

15.   John Daniel MacQueen, son of Donald.

16.   John Smith, Pownal.

17.   Ernest Shaw, son of Allan.

18.   Archibald Macpherson, son of John.

19.   Donald Mor MacLeod, son of Malcolm.

20.   Sir Andrew Macphail, son of William.

21.   Murdoch E. MacLeod, son of Roderick.

24. Daniel, son of Neil Macpherson, and Joseph
     Chisholm, son of Anselm Chisholm.

C.   Joseph McIsaac, cousin of Daniel
     Macpherson.

D.   Wellington MacLeod, Orwell Cove.

SETTLERS
1829

BACK SETTLEMENT (LYNDALE)

Mrs. MacLean
John and Alexander Macdonald
William Gillis
John Beaton
Donald MacIan Oig MacLeod
Murdoch Bruce
Malcolm Lamont
John MacLeod
Murdoch Beaton
John MacLeod
Malcolm Bruce
Archibald Matheson (miller)
Donald Ban Macpherson
Allan Macdonald
Roderick Morrison (first teacher in Lyndale)
John MacArthur

MURRAY HARBOR ROAD

Samuel Martin
Alex. Nicholson
John Martin
Malcolm Macpherson

Donald Ban Oig MacLeod
Archibald, Angus, and Donald MacLeod
(Kinross Corner)
Hector Macdonald
Duncan Macdonald
Martin Martin
Duncan Macdonald
Donald Martin (Orwell Bridge)

Local Place-Names

Uigg, named by the Skye settlers of 1829 after Uig, in Skye. Donald Macdonald, a Skye schoolmaster, who arrived in 1841, and taught in the grammar school, is said to have varied the name to Uigg.

Alberry Plains. This whole district was early swept by fire. After that it was called the Barrens. Following the fire berries grew in abundance. Hence Edward Plaidwell, a U.E. Loyalist, settler in the district, named it Alberry Plains.

Dundee, named by Mary Kettle, wife of John Martin, after her birthplace in Scotland. She arrived in 1842 and died in 1918, aged 94.

Lyndale, named by Ewen Lamont, a Skyeman, at a public meeting called for the purpose, about 1880.

Vernon, is called after Admiral Sir Edward Vernon (1723-1794) uncle of Francis, Lord Orwell. The Admiral used to dilute the sailors' spirits with water in the interests of temperance. He was known as "Old Grog" in allusion to his wearing a grogram coat in foul weather. The watered rum became known as grog.

Orwell, is named after Lord Orwell.

UIGG SCHOOL

In 1906 there was published in the Charlottetown *Guardian* a list of former pupils of the famous Uigg Grammar School, almost all of whom were born in this school district. To this list have been added a few additional names.

LAWYERS:

Malcolm McLeod, K.C., Charlottetown.

Duncan C. McLeod (B.A. McGill), K.C., Charlottetown.

Neil McLeod (M.A. Acadia), County Court Judge, Summerside.

Daniel C. Ross (B.A. McGill, London, Edin.), K.C., Toronto.

Donald A. Mackinnon (LL.B. Dal.), K.C., Charlottetown.

Donald Mackinnon, K.C., Charlottetown.

Malcolm A. Macqueen (B.A. Queen's), Winnipeg.

Alexander R. McLeod (B.A., McGill, Oxon), Vancouver.

MEDICAL DOCTORS:

Hugh Martin (Glas. Univ., New Orleans), Fredericksburg, Va.

Angus McLeod (Harvard), Cambridge, Mass.
James McLeod (McGill), Charlottetown.
William McKinnon, Newfoundland.
Gamaliel Gillis (U. of Penn.), Montague Bridge.
Archibald McLeod (McGill), New Westminster.
William J. Macphail (Wash. D.C.), Orwell.
Sir Andrew Macphail (McGill), Montreal.
Donald McLeod (Trin.), Orwell.
Artemas J. MacKinnon (McGill), Lincoln,
   Neb.
Alexander Ross (Trin.) , Charlottetown.
Isabelle Macphail (Tufts), Orwell.
Charles H. Martin (Boulder Univ.), Idaho.
John J. McPherson (Queen's), Castor, Alta.
Malcolm McKinnon, Heatherdale, P.E.I.
William Judson, Alexandria.

Clergymen:

Donald Gordon Macdonald (Acadia, B.Th.
   McMaster), Vancouver.
J. A. Macdonald, Colorado.
John A. Gordon (M.A., D.D. Acadia),
   Montreal.
John Gillis, Lyndale.
Alexander B. Nicholson (B.A. Queen's, Princ.),
   Prof., Kingston.
Donald M. Campbell (Pine Hill), Saskatoon.

Malcolm C. Martin, Fresno, Cal.

Samuel A. Martin, Churchill, Man.

James Campbell Martin, Roseneath, P.E.I.

Father Kenneth C. McPherson (Laval), Uigg.

Father Pius McDonald (Laval), Glencoe, P.E.I.

Malcolm James McPherson (M.A. Dal., Pine Hill), Uigg.

James A. Crawford (B.A. Dal., Edin.), Cardigan.

Donald McLean, Charlottetown.

James D. McLeod (B.A. Acadia), Uigg.

Fletcher Jordan (B.A. Acadia), Murray Harbor.

Malcolm A. McLean (M.A. Acadia), D.D., Lynchburg, Va.

George B. MacLeod, Toronto.

D. J. MacLeod (M.A., LL.D.), Charlottetown.

ENGINEERS:

(Col.) James Alexander Macphail (McGill), Kingston.

Wm. M. Macphail (McGill), Portland, Oregon.

John Goodwill Macphail (Queen's), Ottawa.

George R. McLeod (McGill), Montreal.

Ernest Jenkins (Queen's), Vancouver.

Aubrey Jenkins (Queen's), Portland, Oregon.

Albert Martin (Dal., Cornell), Montague Bridge.

Murdoch W. McLeod, Dundee (Mechanical).

Daniel W. Musick, Kinross (Mechanical).

School Teachers:

Donald McDonald, Schuyler, Nebraska.
Walter D. Ross (Dal.), Kinross.
Catherine McKinnon.
Christy McKinnon.
Margaret Macphail (Mrs. Albert Jenkins), Orwell.
Katherine Macphail (Mrs. Sam A. Martin), Heatherdale.
Janetta C. Macphail, St. John, N.B.
Bella McLeod (Mrs. Angus Gillis), Victoria Cross.
John Walter McLeod, Vancouver. Annie McLeod, Orwell.
Mary Jane McLeod (Mrs. Rev. D. B. McLeod).
Bella McDonald.
Katherine McLeod.
Christy McLeod (Mrs. Angus McLeod), Oakland, Cal.
Ada Musick (Mrs. J. A. Moore), Pownal.
William H. Musick, Lipton, Sask.
John Gillis, Head Montague.
John Gillis, Kinross.
John Sam-Martin, Uigg.
Catherine Martin (Mrs. Kenneth McLean), Alberry Plains.
Marjorie Martin (Mrs. Lauchlan McKay), Stanley Bridge.
Christy Campbell.

Alex. McKenzie, North River.

Effie McKenzie (Mrs. Capt. Neil Campbell).

Alexander A. Munro, New York.

James A. Campbell (Dal.), Heatherdale.

Mary Campbell (Mrs. Angus Alex. McLeod), Kinross.

John Ross, Hamilton, Ont.

Margaret Ross.

Annabella Ross.

Mary Ross.

Katherine Ross (Mrs. Daniel W. McLeod), Vernon Bridge.

Estelle Jenkins, Vancouver.

Janie Martin, Uigg.

Alexander Robert Macqueen, New Glasgow, N.S.

Peter Alex. Macqueen, Townsville, Australia.

Donald C. MacLeod, Murray Harbor Road.

Donald A. Shaw, Uigg.

Katherine Shaw (Mrs. Angus Martin) Glen Martin.

Donald J. Shaw, Uigg.

Peter Gordon, Uigg.

Alex. McLeod, Athabasca Landing.

Bella McLeod, Vancouver.

John Martin.

Florence McPherson, Uigg.

Ann McLeod (Mrs. Alex. Martin, M.P.) Valleyfield.

Kate McLeod, Uigg.
Duncan Martin, Orwell Head.
Rhy P. McLeod, Uigg.
Katherine A. McLeod (Mrs. Hodgson).
Chester McPherson, Uigg.
Katie McLeod, Uigg.
Haddon Spurgeon McLeod (Guelph Agr. Coll.)
Mary McLeod (Mrs. Dr. McDonald), Calgary.
Mary McPherson, Uigg.
Murdoch G. McLeod, Omaha.
John McKinnon, Uigg.
Margaret McKinnon (Mrs. Geo. H. Brehaut), Little Sands.
Joseph McPherson, Uigg.
Michael McPherson, Uigg.
Roderick Martin, Valleyfield.
Sarah Mutlow, Vancouver.
Ella McLeod, Uigg.
Cyrus McKinnon, Uigg.
Alexander McLeod.
Donald McLeod.
Mrs. McRae, Rice Point.
John McLeod (killed in action in Great War), Kinross.
Mary McLeod (Mrs. Wilfred Furness), Kinross.
Kathleen McLeod, Kinross.
Margaret McLeod, Uigg.

David Douglas Ross, Kinross.
Florence MacLeod, Uigg.
Margaret MacLean.
Malcolm MacLean, Heatherdale.
Norman Campbell, Uigg.
Norman Ross, Uigg.
Alistair MacLeod, Kinross.

DENTIST:

Bruce Findlay, Vancouver.

BANKERS:

James M. Campbell, Ceres, Cal.
John Nicholson, Ellis, Kansas.
Munro MacLeod, Charlottetown.

Through the courtesy of Mr. H. H. Shaw, Chief Superintendent of Education, Charlottetown, the list of teachers who appear on the Government records as having taught in Uigg Grammar School and Orwell School is herewith reproduced. (Before 1849, Angus Martin, and Donald Kelly, taught in Uigg):

	UIGG	ORWELL
1849	Hugh Martin	
1850	Hugh Martin	
1851	Peter Ross	
1852	Alex. McLean	
1855	William Ross	John Brooks
1856	Donald McDonald	John Brooks
1857	Donald McDonald	John Currie
1858	Donald McDonald	John Currie
1859	Donald McDonald	John Currie
1860	Donald McDonald	John Currie
1861	Donald McDonald	Peter McQueen (61-2)
1862	William Macphail	Peter McQueen
1863	William Macphail	Peter McQueen
1864	William Macphail	Martin H. Finlay
1865-66	William Macphail	A. R. McQueen
1867-68	Matt. Dickienson	A. R. McQueen
1869-70	Duncan McLeod	A. R. McQueen
1871-72	Peter Gunn	
1873	D. C. Ross	Flora J. McLeod
1874	D. C. Ross	Finlay D. Martin
1875	Gamaliel Gillis	Miss A. McLeod
1877	D. J. McLeod	John Anderson
1878		Maggie Murchison
1879	John McKinnon	Maggie Murchison
1879	Maggie McPhail	Maggie Murchison

1880	John McKinnon	William McPhail
1880	Maggie McPhail	James H. Campbell
1881	John McKinnon	James H. Campbell
1881	Maggie McPhail	
1882	D. A. McKinnon	Kathleen McLeod
1883	Katie Ross	Kathleen McLeod
1883	D. McLeod	
1884	Katie Ross	
1884	Don. McLeod	John McIsaac
1885	Marjory Martin	
1885	Don. McLeod	Wellington McLaren
1886	Marjory Martin	
1886	D. M. Campbell	Alethe Gunn
1887	Effie McKenzie	
1887	D. M. Campbell	Alethe Gunn
1888	Lizzie McKinnon	
1888	D. M. Campbell	Alethe Gunn
1889	Alex. Ross	
1889	Lizzie McKinnon	
1889	Alex. Ross	James McPhail
1890	Ada Musick	
1890	Donald McDonald	Alex. B. McLean
1891	Ada Musick	
1891	Duncan Martin	A. B. McDonald
1892	G. R. McLeod	Albert J. Fraser
1892	Belle MacLeod	
1893	Geo. R. McLeod	Kenneth McPherson
1893	Christy McLeod	

1894	Kenneth McPherson	Joseph S. O'Neill
1894	Christy McLeod	
1895	Kenneth McPherson	Lizzie Irving
1895	Katie Ross	
1896	M. J. McPherson	Ella McKenzie
1896	Belle McLeod	
1897	M. J. McPherson	J. J. McPherson
1897	Lizzie McKinnon	
1898-99	M. J. McPherson	J. J. McPherson
1898-99	M. A. McQueen	J. J. McPherson
1898-99	Lizzie McKinnon	
1900	W. H. Musick	Ella J. Dorsey
1900	Mary Campbell	
1901	W. H. Musick	A. W. Furness
1901	Mary Campbell	
1902	Ella McLeod	W. E. Jenkins
1902	Mary Campbell	
1903	Alex McLeod	William Musick
1903	D. J. Shaw	
1904	Alex McLeod	W. D. Ross
1904	D. J. Shaw	
1905	Alex McLeod	W. D. Ross
1905	D. J. Shaw	
1906	Alex McLeod	C. McGillivray
1906	Ella McLeod	
1907	J. J. McPherson	John D. McLeod
1907	Ella McLeod	
1908	Jeanette McPhail	Belle McLeod

1908	J. J. McPherson	
1909	Mattie Huntley	
1909	Cordelia Munn	Walter Ross
1910	Rhy P. McLeod	Walter Ross
1910	Cordelia Munn	
1911	M. A. Bears	
1911	Anna McEachern	Blanche Murphy
1912	Eva Carver	
1912	Lou Matheson	Blanche Murphy
1913	Eva Carver	
1913	Mabel McKinnon	Blanche Murphy
1914	Mal. McDonald	
1914	Florence Vickerson	Walter Ross
1915	Mal. E. McDonald	
1915	Florence Vickerson	Gwen McLeod
1916	Mal. E. McDonald	
1916	Florence Vickerson	Estelle Jenkins
1917	Evelyn McLeod	
1917	Nellie Hubley	Estelle Jenkins
1918	Evelyn McLeod	
1918	Estelle Jenkins	Muriel Toombs
1919	Evelyn McLeod	
1919	Ada Campbell	Muriel Toombs
1920	Estelle Jenkins	
1920	Maud McPherson	Florence Ings
1921	Beulah McLeod	
1921	Maud McPherson	Estelle McDonald
1922	Mary McLeod	

1922	Etta K. Thompson	Estelle McDonald
1923	Ada R. Campbell	
1923	Marion Hugh	Walter Ross
1923	Helen Whiteway	
1924	Ruth J. Ross	Blanche Walsh
1924	Chester McPherson	
1925	Marion Hugh	Margaret Scott
1925	Helen Whiteway	
1926	Marion Hugh	Muriel Ross
1926	Kathleen McLeod	
1927	Louis Simmonds	Muriel Ross
1927	Kathleen MacLeod	
1928	Arthur Brooks	Janet Winslow
1928	Kathleen MacLeod	
1929	Florence MacLeod	Florence McPherson
1929	Kathleen MacLeod	

The 1851 Fellowship was won by Col. James A. MacPhail (McGill, Heidelberg). The Gilchrist Scholarship was won by Daniel C. Ross (McGill, Edin., London).

The following resident pupils of Uigg school or descendants of resident pupils won the Rhodes Scholarship:

Alexander R. MacLeod (McGill), barrister, Vancouver.
Norman Robertson (U. of B.C.), professor,

Vancouver. His mother, Floretta McLeod, daughter of Norman "Captain" MacLeod, was born in Uigg school district and attended Uigg school.

Louis Brehaut (Dal.) professor. His mother, Margaret Mackinnon, daughter of William Mackinnon, was born in Uigg school district, and attended Uigg school and later taught there.

Uigg Centennial

The Centennial of the founding of Uigg was celebrated on Saturday, August 17, 1929 on the Uigg
school grounds. Several hundred descendants of
the early pioneers of the district were present to
honor the memory of their ancestors.

Rev. James Campbell Martin, a son of one of the
pioneers acted as chairman and gave an excellent
and scholarly address. He read a letter from Rev.
Donald Gordon Macdonald of Vancouver deplor-
ing his inability to be present and giving a vivid
description of the life of Uigg as he remembers
it over eighty years ago. He referred particularly
to the powerful influence for good exercised by
Rev. Samuel MacLeod.

The chief speaker was Rev. Dr. J. A. Gordon, of
Montreal, who, though eighty-five years of age,
spoke with the fervor of youth. Dr. Gordon's
recital of his boyhood days and his picture of the
pioneer settlers was so unusually graphic and
interesting that a distinguished critic declared it
the best address of the kind he had ever heard.

Sir Andrew Macphail of Montreal, spoke briefly
in terms of deep appreciation of the nobility of
character of the early pioneers and urged the present generation to emulate them.

Rev. Dr. Malcolm A. MacLean of Lynchburg,
Va.; Rev. Henry Pierce of Orwell; John S. Martin

and William MacLeod, Dundas, all stressed the debt the present generation owes their forefathers.

On the following day the Baptist Church, Uigg, was crowded to hear Dr. Gordon, who was assisted by Revs. J. C. Martin, H. Pierce, M. A. MacLean and A. R. MacLeod. Solos were sung by Mrs. Seth Henderson, Mrs. Garrett, Mrs. Vaniderstine and Mrs. Geo. R. MacLeod. These four ladies and the organist Mrs. Walter Scott, all belonged to the fourth generation of their pioneer ancestors.

A few weeks before the incidents above mentioned took place the writer visited Uig, Skye. He was then struck by the great similarity in thought and habits of the two people. A century of separation has not severed the spiritual bonds connecting them. The deeply religious spirit that animated Skye when the Belfast pioneers saw its shores fade away in the distance is the spirit of Skye today. Character now as then is prized as in few other lands. It is only when one visits that misty island that a true measure can be taken of the extraordinary contribution Skye has made to Canada and other lands. Although so small in area, for generations it poured out in a steady stream its sons and daughters for the enrichment of those lands so fortunate as to receive them as settlers. In their adopted homes Skye men and women have stamped the imprint of integrity and fidelity upon the life of the community and have earned for their birthplace fame, and for themselves an enviable reputation for honesty and obedience to law that is the envy of other communities less fortunately endowed.

Although Skye today is reduced to a population barely half of what it was eighty years ago, the quality of those who remain is as high as ever. Sunday is still a day of rest, the Bible is still the oracle of God. The church services are solemn assemblies of the whole people; the sermon, both Gaelic and English, an earnest and moving message. The same insatiable desire for learning that characterized the pioneers of P.E.I. can still be discerned in the place from which they came among even the poorest of the peasants and the fishermen. Among the gentry this is especially the case. Preeminent in pursuing the traditions of the Misty Isle stands Allan R. Macdonald of Waternish. No man alive today knows more of Skye men living and Skye men dead than this profound student of Highland history and tradition. A living bond between the Present and the Past, he is appealed to by Skye men in every clime to unravel the tangled family skeins and is never appealed to in vain. From his unerring hand goes forth such a record of Highland honor and devotion in the Past as ensures its emulation in the Present and its survival in the Future.

The Following
Distinguished Sons and Daughters
of Belfast attended the Belfast Presbyterian
Church

Malcolm James MacLeod (Dal. Princ.), Minister, Collegiate Reformed Church of St. Nicholas, Fifth Ave., N.Y.

Hector MacLeod, banker, Hutchinson, Kansas.

David W. Mackenzie (Dal.), M.D., Royal Vict. Hosp., Montreal.

Ewen Mackenzie (Dal.), Barrister-at-law, Lethbridge.

Harry Mackenzie (Dal.), Barrister-at-law, Charlottetown.

Kenneth J. Martin (Dal.), Barrister-at-law, Charlottetown.

Donald C. Martin (Dal.), ex-M.P., Barrister-at-law, Charlottetown.

Daniel A. Macdonald,* C.J., Court of King's Bench, Manitoba.

Angus A. McLean, Barrister-at-law, ex-M.P., Charlottetown.

---

* Son of Capt. Alexander Macdonald (and his wife, Mary MacRae), son of Hector Macdonald (and his wife, a sister of Angus MacLean), son of Findlay Macdonald, who emigrated to Belfast in 1805 on the brig *Ruther* from Mull, Scotland.

Hector C. Macdonald (McGill), ex-Atty.
Gen. P.E.I., late County Court Judge,
Charlottetown.

Robert Anderson, ex-Mayor of Vancouver.

Angus MacSwain (McGill, Harv., Edin., and
Lond.), M.D., Santa Clara, Cal.

James Nicholson, ex-M.P., Eldon.

John A. Nicholson (McGill), Registrar, McGill
Univ., Montreal.

Daniel Macdonald, M.D., North Pinette.

John D. MacLean (McGill), M.D., ex-Premier
of B.C., Victoria.

Donald A. Macdonald (Dal. and Yale) Minister, Point Prim.

Archibald Murchison, Minister, Point Prim.

John Murchison (Lane Theological Seminary), Point Prim.

Dr. Beaton (Dartmouth), Flat River.

Dr. Riley (U. of Penn.), Flat River.

Daniel McDonald, M.D., New York City.

Whitfield Larrabie (Harvard), M.D., Eldon.

Margaret Eliza Mackenzie (Dal.), M.D.,
Pinette.

Florence McDonald (Trinity), M.D., Pinette.

Annie D. McRae (Trinity), M.D., Pinette.

Annie McRae, M.D., Los Angeles (Ponds,
Belfast).

Roderick C. McRae (Dal.), C.E., Chicago.

Donald McRae, Belfast.

Annie Young, M.D., Pinette, Dean of Schools, Florida.

Kenneth Mackenzie, M.D., Belfast.

Mary Mackenzie (Dal.), Vancouver.

William McLean, Banker, Portage, Belfast.

Alexander McLean (Queens), Minister, Sarnia, Ont.

Angus McLean (U. of Penn.), M.D., Souris East, P.E.I.

J. B. Macdonald (Dal.), Minister, M.D., Pinette.

Charles MacLeod (Dal.), Minister, Eldon.

John McLeod (Dal.), Minister, Surrey.

Donald McLeod (Dal.), Minister, Surrey.

Angus A. Macleod, M.D., Oakland, California.

Donald Sinclair (Dal., Edin.), Minister, Eldon.

Fingal Smith, Cranbrook, B.C., Editor.

Angus A. McLeod, Point Prim, Artist, New York.

Stewart MacMillan, M.D. (Harvard), Belfast.

Ambrose Fraser, Librarian, Charlottetown.

Allan Fraser, Pinette, Minister, Cascumpec.

John MacDougall, M.D., Manitoba.

John MacMillan, M.D., Boston.

Parmenas McLeod (U. of Tor.) Minister, Preeceville, Sask.

Thomas McLeod (B.Sc., McGill).

The Belfast Riot

The first day of March, 1847, has ever been memorable in the history of Belfast, for on that day took place the famous, if unfortunate, Belfast riot.

The following extract from a letter recently received from Mr. A. D. Fraser, librarian, Charlottetown, gives the essential facts of this sad affair:

"I find by reference to the Journals of the House of Assembly and the papers of that period, that the disturbance occurred on Monday, the 1st of March, 1847.

"At the General Election held in August, 1846, Messrs. John McDougall and John Small were declared elected for the Third District (Belfast) of Queen's, and they took their seats when the Assembly met in January (26th), 1847, but a Petition was presented by Messrs. Douse and McLean asking that the election of McDougall and Small be declared void, as there had been intimidation and violence at the Poll. The election was declared void, hence the special election of March 1st, 1847. This election was brought to a sudden close by the Riot, but another election was held on the 19th of March at which Douse (William) and Alex. McLean were duly elected.

"The Irish were the supporters of McDougall and Small, and the Scotch of Douse and McLean.

"You may be aware that the Poll was held a little to the west of Belfast Church on the road leading to Pinette. Malcolm McRae was way-laid and beaten with fatal results, quite near to where the Orange Lodge was situated on the road to Pinette, just below the Belfast Church.

"The Government reports on the matter are very vague. A short Report by the High Sheriff, William Cundall; a Report by Daniel Hodgson, Coroner, and Dr. W. H. Hobkirk, who was sent out to attend the injured. I have never seen anything like an accurate list of the casualties.

"At the election of March 19th there were on hand the 14th Company of Infantry under Captain Dwyer, a Company of Horse under Captain B. Davies, and one hundred and twenty Special Constables.

"On that day William Douse left town at seven a.m., addressed the electors, was elected, returned to town, took his seat in the House and made a speech before five p.m. There was no opposition at this latter election."

(Sgd.) A. D. Fraser,
Librarian.

When the Assembly met in Charlottetown on the 26th day of January, 1847, the members took their seats in that imposing pile, the Colonial Building, at that time not quite completed.

Alexander MacLean, one of the candidates, was from Portage, Belfast. He was commonly known among his Highland neighbors as "Gasda," meaning "goodfellow."

Political passions were greatly aroused. Rev. John MacLennan, minister of the Belfast Presbyterian congregation, and the priest of the adjoining Roman Catholic parish, after consulting together, admonished their respective flocks to exercise forbearance and observe the law.

It was generally understood that an outbreak of lawlessness might occur. The Scots allege that many Irish, who had gathered from distant parts of the province, came armed with clubs. It is also alleged that they started intimidation and coercion as soon as their opponents began to appear. Whatever the facts of the case may be, a party of about twenty Irishmen meeting Malcolm McRae, of Flat River, a native of Applecross, Ross-shire, Scotland, on the road on his way to the Poll, fell upon him with shillelaghs and fractured his skull. He died soon after, in his forty-fourth year. The indignation of the Scottish relatives and neighbors of McRae was extreme. Their Highland passion could not be controlled. They determined at once to avenge this wanton and lawless attack. Couriers on horseback were sent along the road to warn the settlers. "Young" John MacLennan spent the forenoon feverishly preparing sticks with which to arm the Scots. By noon about two hundred had assembled and were armed. A scarf was tied across the shoulder of each to distinguish friend from foe. Thus prepared they lined up near the polling booth. Opposite stood about three hundred similarly armed Irish. Forward both lines swept as if on parade. The clash of stick on stick resounded above the shouts of the warriors. After the melee was over, the Scots remained masters of the field. Many on both sides had received wounds from which they never recovered. The Scots aver that over a dozen Irish were killed on the field, or died shortly after from the effects of wounds. Both sides concealed their losses but it is positively known many on each side were so badly injured that they never fully recovered. Amongst them was William McLeod, of Lyndale, who received head wounds from which he always suffered. Malcolm Campbell, of Uigg, also bore traces of his part in the fray. His stories of the battle, coupled with a ready display of his cranial scars, lent such romance to his presence that he continued to be an ever increasing source of wonder and delight to succeeding generations of schoolboy worshippers.

After the fight was over, better judgment prevailed, and in the intervening eighty years nothing has occurred to mar the cordial relations existing between these kindred races.

Malcolm McRae of Vancouver, grandson of the first, if only, victim of this memorable affray, when recently spoken to in Vancouver, where he resides, stated that as far as the tradition in the McRae family goes, the above is in the main a true outline of the facts of the case.

The strength of some of these Highlanders was prodigious. Rory McLeod, of Pinette, father of Capt. Malcolm McLeod, who died in Vancouver in 1924, was recognized as one of the strongest men in Canada. While yet a boy he gave an exhibition of strength that won him a prize. In a grocery store in Charlottetown he was challenged to exhibit his prowess. He was finally offered a bedtick full of oatmeal as a gift if he could lift it. One of the homemade linen bedticks, manufactured in the hand looms on the farm from native flax, was produced. This was filled with oatmeal, and, thus filled, weighed about twelve hundred pounds. Rory Mor, without hesitation, got under this huge ungainly mass, and with it over his shoulders walked to the dock, from whence he took it by boat to his Belfast home.

He was frequently compared with Angus MacAskill, one of the world's greatest giants.

Born in Harris, Scotland, in 1825, when six years of age he emigrated with his parents, nine sisters, and three brothers, to St. Ann, Victoria Co., Cape Breton Island, N.S., where he was known as Gillie Mor St. Ann. Although his father was only five feet nine inches in height, and his mother an average sized woman, he was seven feet nine inches in height. He was three feet eight inches across the shoulders. The palm of his hand was six inches wide and twelve inches long. He wore a shoe eighteen inches in length. His strength was enormous. In disengaging himself from an anchor of tremendous weight, which he had lifted to his shoulder, he received an injury from the effects of which he ultimately died. This man only, would the Belfast people admit, was more powerful than Rory McLeod of Pinette, their hero.

Part Three: Belfast Families

The Munros
of Orwell, Alberry Plains, and Lorne Valley

It is believed that the ancestors of this family emigrated from Caithness or adjoining county, to Skye, at an early period. George Munro, the "fair miller," or "miller of Strath," in Skye, is believed to have married Jessie Nicholson, with issue, among others:

I.   Andrew, an officer in the naval service, taken prisoner by the Barbary pirates, escaped and subsequently went to South America.

II. John, married Fanny, daughter of Capt. Kenneth Macdonald of Cuidrach, living in 1842 at Grantown, Inverness-shire, with issue, among others:

  1. Andrew, at that date serving with his regiment at Cape of Good Hope, and on August 13, 1862, living with his mother and his aunt, Mary Macdonald, in Forres, Scot.

  2. George, married to Miss Donaldson, with issue: four sons and three daughters, living on August 13, 1862, and for thirty years prior thereto, in Dundee, Scotland.

  3. Kenneth, married, with issue, living

in Grantown, Strathspey, Scotland, in
August, 1862.

III. JAMES, born in Skye in or about 1768. In 1785
and 1786 he entered as a medical student at
the University of Edinburgh, and took classes
in Chemistry, Anatomy, Surgery and Practical
Medicine. The complete course of medical
instruction at Universities and Colleges in
Scotland at that time was two years. There
was no Medical Licensing Board regulating
who should practice medicine, and anyone
could practice that profession, male or female,
trained or untrained. Not until 1858 was there
state supervision of Medicine. After that no
unqualified person could pose as a "Doctor."
In 1786 he began the practice of his profession in his native Isle in "Sleat, Strath and the
Braes of Troderniss." He later moved to Uig,
in the Parish of Kilmuir, where he resided
until July 14, 1840, when, with his wife Annabella Macleod, and family, and nephew,
Thomas Boston Munro, he sailed on the Brig
Ruther, 273 tons, of Sunderland, for P.E.I. He
contracted pneumonia, and was put ashore
at Tobermory, where he died. His wife and
two daughters, Jacobina and Margaret Alice,
who stayed with him, rejoined the rest of the
family in Orwell, in 1841. They took up land
and settled in Alberry Plains. Their issue were:

1. MARION, b. 1812, d. June, 1897. In 1842 married Peter Nicholson, miller, Orwell, with issue.
2. GEORGE, b. 1815, emigrated to Australia about 1855.
3. DONALD, b. 1819, d. Alberry Plains, Oct. 8, 1884. Began an incompleted medical course in Scotland. For years there was no physician in his district on P.E.I. During this period he devoted himself to healing and helping his neighbors. To them he was known as "Doctor" Munro. He represented the Belfast district in Queen's County in the P.E.I. legislature, and was Lieutenant-Colonel of the Third (or Highland) Regiment of Queen's County Militia. He is buried in Belfast churchyard.

    As a family the Munros for generations were noted for their fair complexion, fine physique, and handsome presence. In these particulars Donald Munro was no exception. He had a high reputation among the early settlers for skill in treating nervous disorders. By nature sympathetic, he always lent an attentive ear to his patient's troubles, even if obviously imaginary. On one occasion, one of his Point Prim patients in his distress conceived the idea that he harbored a live rat in his stomach. Such beliefs were not uncommon in those days. Doctor Munro agreed with this diagnosis. He made arrangements suitable to the needs of the case, and after the afflicted one had undergone a paroxysm of nausea, produced a rat before the eyes of the astonished sufferer. So beneficial was the treatment that the patient soon arose from his sick bed completely restored to good health.

Mr. Munro married Jessie, sister of Senator Dr. Robertson, b. 1833, in New Perth, d. May 1, 1910, with issue:

a. JAMES, b. 1887, d. May 28, 1899, unmarried.

b. ANNA, b. 1865, d. 1926, unmarried.

c. MARGARET, d. Oct. 22, 1911, wife of Capt. John Nicholson, of Orwell Cove, d. Oct., 1927, with issue:

   (1) Angus (B.A., U. of Sask.) b. Feb. 13, 1895, Lieut. 16th Canadian Scottish—killed in action, Flanders, March 5, 1918.

   (2) Jessie.

   (3) Alice.

   (4) John.

d. NELLIE, b. 1867, wife of Hiram Campbell, Wrangel, Alaska, with issue:

   (1) Leonard.

(2) Ernest, the latter married with issue:

(a) Leonard.

e. Alice, wife of Clarence Stewart, Little Harbor, N.S.

f. George, b. 1872, d. April 24, 1900, married, without issue.

g. Jessie, b. 1875, wife of Murdoch A. Macleod, Dundee, P.E.I., with issue; 2nd, Rev. Dr. Genge.

4. Malcolm James, b. about 1822, d. 1849 or 1850, in New Orleans, unmarried.

5. Jessie Elizabeth, b. Uig, Kilmuir, Skye, 1824, d. Jan., 1904, wife of Malcolm MacLeod, Murray Harbor Road, without issue, buried in Orwell Head churchyard.

6. Jacobina Annabella, b. Uig, Skye, 1831, d. 1911, wife of her distant relative, Charles Crawford, Cardigan, with issue surviving:

a. Rev. James Crawford (B.A. Dal., Pine Hill, Edin.), b. 1864, Fintray, Aberdeenshire, married Blanche, daughter of Rev. J. R. Munro, Pictou Co., N.S., with issue:

(1) Mary Munro, b. 1912.

(2) Annabella Margaret, b. 1914.

b. Amram George, b. 1871, married Eva Bulpitt, b. 1872, with issue:

(1) Marion Eliza, b. 1907.

(2) Deborah Mildred, b. 1908.

(3) James, b. 1910.

(4) Blanche Munro, b. 1912.

(5) Charles, b. 1914.

c. SARAH ANNE, b. 1854, d. 1882, wife of John Williams, with issue:

(1) Almira, married, with issue, living in Vermont.

7. MARGARET ALICE, b. 1836, Uig, Skye, d. South Edmonton, Dec. 24, 1912, wife of Donald Macdonald, b. Skye, 1825, d. Dec. 24, 1911, with issue surviving:

a. JOHN, b. June, 1858, Witten, South Dakota, married Helen Bruce, Aberdeen, Scotland, with issue.

b. ALEXANDER, b. Sept., 1863, Fort Saskatchewan, Alberta, married Lucy Kephart, 1913, with issue.

c. PETER NICHOLSON, b. May, 1866, Bloomfield, Nebraska, married Maria Mitchell, with issue.

d. KATHERINE, b. April, 1868, Seattle, Washington.

e. ISABELLA MARION, b. May, 1870, d. Sept., 1915, wife of Robert Carpenter, Creighton, Nebraska, with issue.

f. GEORGE ROBERT GREY, b. Aug., 1872, Billings, Montana.

IV. ALEXANDER MUNRO (*Alasdair Mor na h'urnuigh,*[*]
Big Alexander of the Prayers), was born in
Kilmuir, Skye, in 1774; Gaelic schoolmaster
from May 1, 1821, to November 1, 1832, at
Fernlea, Minginish, Parish of Bracadale, Skye,
and thereafter to May 1, 1838, at Shawbost,
Parish of Lochs, Lewis. He was employed in
this work by the Honorable Society in Scotland for Propagating Christian Knowledge.
During the same period he was catechist, and
like his famous cousin, Blind Donald Munroe,
catechist, was noted for religious zeal. He
emigrated to P.E.I. with his family in 1842,
and settled in Brown's Creek (Valleyfield),
where he taught school and preached. A few
years later he moved to Head of Cardigan
(Lorne Valley), and there he passed away on
November 11, 1856. His wife was Euphemia
Campbell, cousin of Sir Colin Campbell. She
died at Lorne Valley about 1882, aged 93 years.
Both are buried in the Valleyfield churchyard.
Their issue were:
1.   JANET, wife of Angus McFarlane, Skye.
2.   THOMAS BOSTON MUNRO, b. Triaslan, Skye,
     Oct.17, 1817, d. Nebraska, June 31, 1888;
     schoolmaster, Shawbost, Skye; arrived
     in Charlottetown on Brig *Ruther*, Sept. 8,

---

[*]   *The Men of Skye,* by Robert McCowan.

1840; taught school on P.E.I. 1841 to 1870; married Sarah Shaw, Flat River, b. Oct. 16, 1827, d. Nebraska, Dec. 20, 1897; preached in Dundas and Brown's Creek; both buried in Irvington, Douglas Co., Nebraska; their issue were:

a.   JANET, b. Dec. 16, 1852, d. Seattle, June 4, 1913, wife of James Burns, with issue.

b.   ALEXANDER A., b. June 18, 1854 (M.A., U. of Neb., Columbia, Ph.D., U. of Wis.), Supt. of Schools, Omaha, 1887 to 1898, Principal in Schools, N.Y. City, married Mary Spaulding, b. Jan. 14, 1869, with issue:

(1) Thomas Munro, b. Feb. 15, 1897 (Ph.D. Columbia), Prof. of Philosophy, Rutgers Univ., Lecturer in Fine Arts, N.Y. Univ., married Lucile Nadler, with issue:

(a) Eleanor Carroll, b. Mar. 28, 1928.

c.   EUPHEMIA, b. Sept. 2, 1857, wife of John S. Craig, with issue, among others:

(1) John Craig, b. Sept. 13, 1880, Attorney at Law, Council Bluffs, Iowa, Lieut. A. E. F., married Hattie Hains.

d.   ALLAN, b. April 29, 1859, Kent, Washington.

e.   GEORGE A., b. Aug. 15, 1862, d. Oct., 1914 (U. of Neb.), minister, Congregational Church, Nebraska and Colorado, married, with issue, among others:

    (1) Charles D., financial agent, Los Angeles.

    (2) Bessie, wife of Rev. Herman Lindeman, Yankton, S. Dakota.

    (3) Everett H., physician, Grand Junction, Colorado.

    (4) Robert Blair, Grand Junction, civil engineer.

    (5) George A., attorney at law, Kearney, Neb., married, with issue, among others:

       (a) Nancy Jean.

f.   DONALD, b. May 27, 1864, d. Alberta, Feb. 17, 1899.

g.   CATHERINE ELIZABETH, b. April 19, 1867, d. Seattle, 1923, married, with issue.

3. GEORGE, b. 1821, married, first Louise Swan, Little York, with issue, among others:

a.   KATHERINE EUPHEMIA, Moose Jaw, married John Macdonald, without issue.

b.   HATTIE WADMAN, Crapaud, with issue.

4. FLORA, wife of Neil Shaw, Lorne Valley, with issue, among others:
   a. ALLAN SHAW, Cardigan.
5. CATHERINE, d. July 26, 1854, wife of John Shaw, Lorne Valley, with issue:
   a. EUPHEMIA, wife of Mr. Scribner, Mich., U.S.A.
   b. KATHERINE, wife of Murdoch Nicholson, Lorne Valley.
   c. ALEXANDER, married, with issue, the latter, while Master of the barque *Veronica* in 1902, was murdered on the the High Seas, under atrocious circumstances, by members of a mutinous crew.[*]
6. JOHN, b. Skye, May 1831, d. Lorne Valley, Jan. 10, 1917, schoolmaster, catechist, and farmer, married Jane MacSwain, b. Skye, emigrated to P.E.I. 1840, d. Mar. 13, 1925, with issue:
   a. CATHERINE, b. Feb. 23, 1861, wife of Eben Finlayson, Riverton, without issue.
   b. EUPHEMIA CATHERINE, b. April 19, 1864, Lorne Valley.
   c. GEORGE ANDREW, Brookville, Pa., b. Mar. 4, 1866, married, with issue.

---

[*] *In the Wake of the Wind Ships,* by F. W. Wallace.

d. JAMES ALLAN, Barrister, Moose Jaw, b. Sept. 7, 1868, d. May 3, 1920, unmarried.

e. ANNABELLA, b. June 18, 1870, d. Aug. 21, 1898, wife of Charles McGrath, with issue, among others:
   (1) Kimpton.
   (2) Munro.

f. DONALD, b. July 2, 1872, Sacramento, Cal., married, with issue.

g. MARY, b. May 18, 1876, d. Jan. 20, 1927, wife of Daniel MacSwain, Lorne Valley, with issue.

h. JACOBINA, b. May 12, 1878, wife of George Howard Lydiard, Moose Jaw, Sask., with issue:
   (1) John Munro.
   (2) Jean Munro.
   (3) George Edward.
   (4) Mary Euphemia.

i. ALEXANDER, b. July 5, 1882, Queen Charlotte Island.

7. ANNE, b. 1834, d. 1926, wife of John McSwain, Lorne Valley, with issue: eight children.

8. MARY, b. 1834, wife of Capt. Allan Mac-Swain; lives in Lorne Valley, without issue. Anne and Mary were twins.

9. DONALD, married Catherine Cameron,

Whim Road Cross, with issue.
10. CHRISTY, wife of Neil MacLeod, without
    issue.

The Munros of Lyndale are connections of the
above family. Donald Munro emigrated to that
district in 1840 from Kilmuir, Skye. He died on
May 24, 1873, aged 80, and is buried in the Baptist
churchyard at Uigg. He was succeeded on the
Lyndale homestead by his son Roderick, b. 1837,
d. 1912. He left a large family. A son lives on
the old farms. Daughters are married to: Daniel
Alexander Macpherson, merchant, Uigg; Neil
George Macpherson, Newtown; and William Bec
MacLeod, Orwell Cove. Others left the district.

Another branch of the same family are the Munros
of Kilmuir, P. E. Island.

Certificates were given Dr. James Munro, on leaving Skye for "The Island."

That the bearer, Surgeon James Munro, has
long practised in this country in that capacity
and has for several years been in the commission of Peace as one of the Justices for the
County of Inverness; that he always adhered
to the Prebyterian form of worship as followed
in the Church of Scotland — that he has been

known to me from my infancy, and that as a member of society, and a gentleman of the strictest integrity, he has been always esteemed in this country, and in this parish is certified at Snizort, this 10th day of July, 1840, by

(Sgd.) Rodk. McLeod, Minister of Snizort
(Sgd.) D. Daly, Lt.-Gov. By His Excellence Dominick Daly, Esq., Lieut-Governor and Commander-in Chief, in and over her Majesty's Island, Prince Edward, Vice-Admiral and Ordinary of the same, etc., etc., etc.

To Donald Munro (Gentleman) Greeting:

By virtue of the power and authority in me vested, I do, by these presents, constitute and apppoint you Lieutenant-Colonel of the Third (or Highland) Regiment of the Queen's County Militia.

You are therefore carefully and diligently to discharge the duty of Lieutenant-Colonel by doing and performing any and all manner of things hereunto belonging; and you are to observe and follow such orders and directions, from time to time, as you shall receive from me, or any other your Superior Officer, according to the Rules and Discipline of War, and the Laws of this Island, in pursuance of the trust hereby reposed in you.

Given under my Hand and Seal at Ams, in
Charlottetown, Prince Edward Island,
the Eighth day of November, 1855, in the
Nineteenth year of the Reign of Her Majesty,
Queen Victoria. By His Excellency's Command.
(Sgd.) GEORGE COLES
Col. Secretary
Entered with the Adjutant-General the ___
day of November, 1855.

To The Independent Electors Of The Third District of King's County

Gentlemen:

In compliance with the repeated solications
of many of yourselves, I beg to offer my services as a candidate for the representation in
your District in the next House of Assembly.

Having resided in your midst for the last
twenty years, it is neeedless for me to enter
into any explanation of my political views; you
know, Gentlemen, that I have always been an
advocate of Liberal principles—When I had the
honor of a seat in the Legislature as one of the
Representatives for Belfast District, I always
gave my vote in favor of every measure of
Reform brought under the consideration of
the House of Assembly. I am opposed to any

scheme of Confederation that would include Prince Edward Island—believing as I do that our interests are better served in our present position and relation with the Mother Country.

I have only to add, Gentlemen, that should you confer on my the high honor of electing me as one of your Representatives, I will do all in my honor to further the interests of your District and the Island generally.

I have the honor to be, Gentlemen,

Your obedient servant,

DONALD MUNRO

Georgetown Road, February 1st, 1867

FAMILY OF
DR. ANGUS MACAULAY, POINT PRIM

Aeneas Macaulay's birthplace is not known definitely, but it is believed to have been Skye or Lewis. It is probable that he was kinsman of Lord Macaulay, and also of the famous Lewis family to which belongs the great captain of finance, T. B. Macaulay, President of the Sun Life Assurance Company of Canada.

Aeneas Macaulay was graduated A.M. by the University of Glasgow, and later took a course in Theology, probably in the same institution. For some years he was Chaplain to the 1st West India Regiment. Later he took up the study of Medicine in his Alma Mater, and in January, 1803, was graduated M.D. by that University.

When the Earl of Selkirk undertook his scheme of colonization in Prince Edward Island he chose Aeneas Macaulay his Factor, and in that capacity he accompanied the immigrants who arrived in the Belfast district in 1803. On the voyage he was ship's surgeon on the *Polly*. From the first Doctor Macaulay employed all his skill and strength in an effort to improve the lot of his neighbors and friends in the new settlement, and by them he was looked upon as a wise counsellor and faithful friend. In as far as he could he endeavored to ameliorate their position. His compassionate nature is

proven by a letter from the proprietor chiding him
for being too easy with the tenants in collecting
the rents. He took a leading part not only in local,
but also in the larger affairs of the whole Island.
In 1818 he was Speaker of the provincial house. In
1825 he was leader in the movement for Catholic
Emancipation and Reform. Nothing could better
show the tolerance of this Presbyterian minister
and the Highlanders among whom he lived, than
his stand on these contentious matters.

Prince Edward Island owes much to Dr.
Macaulay and his wife, and their memory is not
forgotten to this day by the descendants of the
settlers of 1803.

The Doctor received a grant of eleven hundred
and two acres of land in the Point Prim district,
from Lord Selkirk. Some of this is occupied by
his descendants at the present time.

The wife of Dr. Aeneas Macaulay was Mary
Macdonald, daughter of Captain Samuel Macdonald of Sartle, in Skye, who was born about 1739,
and died 10th October, 1830. "Captain Samuel,"
as he was always known, was a son of Alexander
Macdonald, of the Ardnamurchan family, who
occupied Sartle in 1733, and his wife Margaret,
daughter of Somerled ("Soirle") Macdonald of
Sartle, fourth son of Sir James Macdonald, second
Baronet of Sleat. Donald, a brother of Samuel,
occupied Boronos Kitag and Glensdall. Samuel

Macdonald emigrated to Carolina in 1770, and on the breaking out of the Revolutionary War joined the Loyalists, and served under Allan Macdonald, husband of the celebrated Flora Macdonald. In the battle of Widow Moore's Creek Bridge he was taken prisoner. Being exchanged he rejoined the Army. In 1787 he was in Shelburne, N.S. Shortly afterwards he returned to Skye a ruined man, but with the rank and half pay of a Lieutenant. He acquired Sartle after his return and lived there for many years. On leaving Sartle for Quinto-lan, the old place was acquired by John Graham, husband of Susan Martin, who was grandniece of the old Captain. The mother of the Martins of Beallach, viz:—Martin Martin, who was married to a daughter of Macleod of Raasay, and the father of the late Mrs. Martin, Tote House; the Rev. Donald Martin, Rev. Lachlan Martin (grandfather of Dr. L. M. Matheson) and Rev. Angus Martin— was a daughter of said Alexander Macdonald of Sartle. Captain Macdonald was a man of gigantic frame and herculean strength. When he was about ninety years old he married Catherine Stewart, then twenty-two years of age, who died in Kilvax-ter in 1886. She was a relation of his own. By this union there were three children. On the mother's side she was niece of Adjutant Eon Macdonald, of Lord Macdonald's Regiment, who latterly had a house and lands in Bernisdale. The Adjutant's grandfather on the mother's side was Eon Mor, who walked from Edinburgh to Kilmuir, Skye, in three days, and, before partaking of any kind of refreshment (for he was under a vow), thrashed a bully who had maltreated a nephew of his.

The said Alexander Macdonald's wife, Margaret, was sister of Captain Hugh Macdonald of Armadale, stepfather of the celebrated Flora. Mrs. Macaulay was therefore cousin of Annabella Macleod, wife of Dr. James Munro, who settled with his family in the Orwell and Alberry Plains district, in 1840 and 1841. She died April 9th, 1857, aged ninety-nine, and is buried beside her husband in the Mount Buchanan cemetery, Belfast, which he had donated for the purpose of a graveyard.

Dr. and Mrs. Macaulay had six children who reached maturity:

I.   CHARLOTTE, wife of Angus MacLean, Point Prim, with issue:
    1.   MARY, married.
    2.   MARGARET, wife of Malcolm MacLeod, Glashvin.
    3.   ANGUS, unmarried.
II. FLORA, unmarried.
III. JOHN, unmarried.
IV. WILLIAM, Wisconsin, married Miss Henderson, Ontario, with issue: one daughter.

V. Eben, unmarried, died aged 22.
VI. Alice, wife of Samuel Murchison, Pinette, with issue reaching maturity:
    1. Charlotte, unmarried.
    2. Mary, wife of Donald McLeod, Mount Buchanan, with issue:
        a. Anne, wife of Donald McKay, Montague Bridge.
        b. Alice, wife of John Martin, Whim Road.
        c. Flora, wife of John McKinnon, Point Prim.
        d. Malcolm, Master Mariner, married Catherine McDonald, Point Prim.
        e. Alexander, Master Mariner, married Margaret Murchison, Point Prim.
        f. Mary Anne, married Samuel Murchison, Pinette.
    3. Catherine, wife of Walter Ross, Eldon, with issue.
    4. Angus Macaulay, married Catherine, daughter of Roderick Mackinnon, with issue who reached maturity:
        a. Alice.
        b. John.
        c. Laughlan.
        d. Samuel, Contractor, Vancouver, married Mary Anne MacLeod, with issue:
            (1) Alice.

(2) Mary Kathleen, wife of Leonard John Hovington, Honolulu.

e. Catherine, wife of James Fraser, Eldon, with issue:

(1) John Murchison.

(2) Alice, wife of George L. Telfer, New York.

f. Malcolm William, Pinette, married Margaret MacDonald, with issue:

(1) Alice.

(2) Roderick.

(3) Angus.

They live on the ancestral homestead.

g. Roderick, Master Mariner.

h. Flora Margaret.

i. Neil Alexander.

x. Mary.

xi. Angus.

The MacKinnons of Uigg

The Mackinnons were one of the powerful clans in Skye. Among the Uigg settlers of 1829 were Malcolm Mackinnon and his wife, formerly Miss Campbell, both from Skye. They had issue, among others:

I.   ALEXANDER, d. Mar. 5, 1887, aged 68, married Jessie Macdonald, Uigg, d. Jan. 30, 1899, aged 79, with issue:
  1. ARCHIBALD, married, without issue.
  2. MARY, wife of Donald Nicholson.
  3. ANGUS, unmarried.
  4. CATHERINE, wife of Alexander MacLeod, Jr., Master Mariner, Orwell, with issue.
  5. MARGARET, wife of Mr. Coles, Gardiner, Maine, with issue.
  6. ANNE, wife of Mr. Murray, Lynn, Mass., with issue.
II. WILLIAM, married Katherine Nicholson, Orwell Cove, sister of Angus Nicholson, with issue:
  1. DONALD A., b. Feb. 21, 1863, d. April 20, 1928, K.C., M.P., Lieut.-Gov., P.E.I., married Miss Owen, Georgetown, with issue:
    a. BEATRICE.
    b. ARTHUR.
  2. BELLA, wife of Alexander Bruce, Valleyfield, with issue, among others:

a. Malcolm, M.L.A.
3. Margaret, wife of George Hammond
    Brehaut, Little Sands, with issue:
    a. Ernest (M.A., Dal., Ph.D., Col.).
    b. Alder (LL.B., Dal.).
    c. Cora (B.A., McGill).
    d. Hammond (B.A., Dal.).
    e. Lester (M.D., Dal.)
    f. Louis (B.A., Dal., Oxon.).
    g. Elsie.
    h. John.
    i. Louise.
4. Charles, b. Aug. 10, 1858, d. Oct. 28, 1911,
    married Mary Dockerty, d. Feb. 11, 1912,
    aged 46, Victoria Cross, with issue:
    a. Florence.
    b. William, twin of Florence.
    c. Jean.
    d. Louise.
5. Artemas (M.D., McGill), Omaha,
    Nebraska.
6. Elizabeth, b. Nov. 18, 1865, d. April 25,
    1907, wife of Murdoch E. MacLeod, Uigg,
    with issue.
7. John, unmarried, deceased.
8. Malcolm, unmarried, deceased.

ANCESTORS AND DESCENDANTS OF
ANNABELLA MACLEOD
WIFE OF DR. JAMES MUNRO
THROUGH THE MACDONALDS, LORDS OF THE ISLES

1. Somerled, married Raguhildis.
2. Reginald, married Fonia.
3. Donald, married daughter of Walter, Steward of Scotland.
4. Sir Angus Mor de Yle, married daughter of Sir Colin Campbell.
5. Angus de Yle, married Agnes O'Cahan.
6. John de Yle, married Margaret, daughter King Robert II.
7. Donald, married Mary Leslie.
8. Alexander de Yle.
9. Hugh Alexander, II Baron of Sleat, married Elizabeth Gunn.
10. Donald Gallach, III Baron of Sleat, married Agnes.
11. Donald Gruamach, IV Baron of Sleat, married Catherine MacDonald.
12. Donald Gorm, V Baron of Sleat, married Margaret MacLeod.
13. Donald Gormson, VI Baron of Sleat, married Mary MacLean.
14. Archibald Macdonald.
15. Sir Donald Macdonald, first Baronet of Sleat, married Janet Mackenzie.

16. Sir James Macdonald, second Baronet of Sleat, married Margaret Mackenzie.
17. Somerled Macdonald, married Mary MacLeod.
18. Hugh Macdonald, married Marion Macdonald.
19. Annabella Macdonald, married Alexander Macdonald.
20. Marion Macdonald, married Murdoch MacLeod.
21. Annabella MacLeod, married James Munro.
22. Marion Munro, married Peter Nicholson.
23. Isabella Nicholson, married John A. Macqueen.
24. James, Matilda, Malcolm and Peter Macqueen.

1. The Great Somerled, "Rex Insularum," Thane of Argyle, took up arms against Malcolm IV, King of Scotland. After a war of three years, peace was established in 1157. In 1164 Somerled renewed hostilities and invaded the mainland with a large army. He was assassinated at Renfrew by a bribed miscreant named Maurice MacNeil, a relative of Somerled, who had no fear of his presence in camp. Somerled was married to Raguhildis, daughter of Olave the Black, King of Man.

2. Reginald, described in his charter (about 1180) to Paisley Abbey as "Reginaldus Filius Somerled Dominus de Inchegal." His seal to this charter is inscribed, "Reginaldus Rex Insularum, Dominus de Ergile." Reginald was

married to Fonia, granddaughter of Fergus, Prince of Galloway.

3. Donald, in his charter to the monastery of Paisley, about 1210, was described as "Dovenaldus filius Reginaldi filii Somerled dominus de Inchegal." He was married to a daughter of Walter, Steward of Scotland, by his wife, Marjory, daughter of King Robert the Bruce.

4. Sir Angus Mor de Yle, Lord of the Isles, was son of Donald, Lord of Inchegal. He married a daughter of Sir Colin Campbell of Lochawe.

5. Angus de Yle, Lord of the Isles, was the second son of Sir Angus Mor. (The eldest son, Alexander de Yle, was forfeited by Robert the Bruce for siding with the Balliol party against him.) Angus was the staunch friend of Bruce in his misfortunes, and did yeoman service in the final struggle at Bannockburn. He was married to Agnes, daughter of Guy O'Cahan of Ulster.

6. John de Yle, Lord of the Isles, was son of said Angus and Agnes. His second wife was Margaret, daughter of King Robert II. Being cousins, Papal dispensation was granted to permit them to marry. "To the Bishop of St. Andrews, mandate to dispense John de Insulis, Lord of the Isles, and Margaret, daughter of Robert, called Stewart, Knight, of the diocese of Glasgow, so as to intermarry, they

being related in the third and fourth degree of affinity" (18 Kalands, July, 1350, Avignon).

7.   Donald, Lord of the Isles, was eldest son of said John and Margaret. He was a renowned chieftain, and led the Highland hosts in the famous battle of Harlaw. His wife was Mary, in her own right Countess of Ross, daughter of Sir Walter Leslie, by Euphemia, Countess of Ross.

8.   Alexander de Yle, Earl of Ross, and Lord of the Isles, was the son of said Donald and Mary.

9.   Hugh Alexander, son of Alexander de Yle, succeeded his half brother John, I Baron of Sleat. From him he received a charter in 1469 of the lands of Sleat and Uist. (Dispensation by Pope Eugenius IV in favour of Hugh Alexander and Donald, sons of Alexander de Yle, Earl of Ross, legitimating them—the illegitimate sons of the said Alexander de Yle, Earl of Ross, a married man and an unmarried woman.) He married Elizabeth Gunn, daughter of the Crowner of Caithness, and had among other issue:

10. Donald Gallach, III Baron of Sleat, son of Hugh Alexander and Elizabeth. He married Agnes, daughter of Sir John of the Isles (called Cathanac), Lord of Dunnyveg and the Glens. They were succeeded by their son:

11. Donald Gruamach, IV Baron of Sleat. Next

to Macdonald of Islay, he was the most prominent chieftain of his race in his day. "Donald the Grim despised the peaceful art of the clerk, and when along with other chiefs he signed a bond of offence and defence (at Inverness) on the 30th April, 1527, it was with his 'hand at the pen guided by Sir William Munro, notary public.'" He died in 1534. He married Catherine, daughter of the Captain of Clanranald.

12. Donald Gorm, V Baron of Sleat, was son of Donald Gruamach, by his wife Catherine. The chiefs of Sleat now took up their abode in the castle of Duntulm. His claim to the lordship of the Isles, and to the earldom of Ross, was disputed by Mackenzie of Kintail. He ravaged Mackenzie's lands and besieged him in his castle before which he received an arrow wound in the foot, from which he died in 1539. His wife was Margaret, daughter of Siol Torquil MacLeod of the Lewis.

13. Donald Gormson (Sassunach), VI Baron of Sleat, was son of Donald Gorm. He "was a minor of tender years" when he succeeded his father. He died in 1585. His wife was Mary, daughter of Hector Mor MacLean of Duart. Their eldest son, Donald Gorm Mor, succeeded as VII Baron of Sleat. He died in December, 1616.

14. Archibald, second son of Donald Gormson, married. His son was:

15. Sir Donald Macdonald (Donald Gorm Oig), first Baronet of Sleat, died in October, 1643. He married Janet, daughter of Kenneth, first Lord Mackenzie of Kintail, sister of Colin and George, first and second Earls of Seaforth.

16. Sir James Macdonald, second Baronet, eldest son of Sir Donald, succeeded his father. He joined Montrose in 1645. After the defeat of the King's forces at Worcester in 1651, he retired to Skye, "where he lived with great circumspection" until his death on December 8, 1678. His first wife was Margaret, daughter of Sir Roderick Mackenzie of Tarbat, ancestor of the Earls of Cromarty.

17. Somerled "Soirlee" Macdonald of Sartle was fourth son of Sir James, by his first wife, Margaret. He married Mary, daughter of Murdo MacLeod, called "Tutor" of Raasay.

18. Captain Hugh Macdonald* of Armadale, was third son of Somerled. In 1728 he abducted and married Marion Macdonald, widow of Ranald Macdonald II, of Milton, South Uist, the mother, by her first husband, of the

---

*   Emigrated to North Carolina about 1771 or 1772 where he died 1780. In addition to Annabella and others, he had a son James, a lieutenant in the Dutch service 1747-8.

celebrated Flora Macdonald. Capt. Hugh was one of the most powerful men of his clan. Being blind of an eye, he was known as Uisdean Cam. It was he who, while in command of a body of militia in Uist, furnished his stepdaughter, Flora, with a passport for herself, "Betty Burke" (the Prince) and crew, to pass the Minch to Skye.

19. Annabella Macdonald, daughter of Capt. Hugh and Marion, married Major Alexander Macdonald of Cuidrach, Skye, a descendant of Hugh Macdonald, fourth son of Domhnull Mac Ian'ic Sheumais, a "distinguished warrior of unsurpassed courage and enormous strength," third of Kingsburgh. In or about 1772, they joined the great Macdonald migration to the Carolinas.

After the Revolutionary War broke out, agents of the British government recruited the Royal Highland Emigrant Regiment, numbered the 84th, in the Highland settlements in Carolina. Allan Macdonald, husband of Flora, was Brigade Major. Alexander Macdonald, of Cuidrach, served as Major under him. Despite the lessons of the "forty-five," when she found herself a prisoner in the Tower of London, Flora threw her powerful and ill-fated influence among the clansmen, on the side of reaction. She exerted herself to gain recruits. Mounted on a white charger she rode before, and animated the assembled troops by a stirring address in Gaelic.

In February, 1776, the regiment started its march from Cross Creek to Brunswick, N.C., to embark for Halifax, Nova Scotia. On February 27, 1776, at Widow Moore's Creek Bridge, the Highland Army, eighteen hundred strong, was met by the insurgents and scattered. With grim irony, almost all the officers soon found themselves prisoners in Halifax, Virginia, instead of in the Halifax for which they started. Major Allan, his son Lieut. Alexander, and Major Alexander of Cuidrach, were exchanged in the autumn of 1777, and after serving in New York until the end of 1778, Majors Allan and Alexander rejoined their regiment in Nova Scotia, where they remained on duty until the regiment was disbanded in 1783. They then returned to Skye, where Flora and her daughters had gone in 1779. Annabella and her five children returned from Carolina to London in 1781. In addition to her husband, Flora had five sons in the war, all officers.

In the memorable Battle of the Saints, or "Glorious 12th of April," 1782, Compte de Grasse surrendered his flagship *Ville de Paris* to the immortal Rodney. She was the finest and largest first-rate line-of-battle ship in the world, the gift of the citizens of Paris to Louis XIV. She had thirteen hundred men on board in the battle, hundreds of whom were soldiers. From three hundred to four hundred were dead or wounded when the fight was over.

In the summer of 1782, the *Ville de Paris* started for England in convoy. There were upwards of five hundred men on board. The prize crew was under command of Flora's son, Ranald, Captain of Marines, who was wounded on the *Princessa* in the battle. With him was his brother, Lieut. Alexander, who had joined the ship shortly prior thereto. In mid ocean, on September 14, 1782, she was struck by a terrific hurricane and foundered. All on board were lost.

Flora's son, Charles, a Captain in the Queen's Rangers, under Col. Simcoe; Captain James, "a brave officer who served with distinction" in Tarleton's British Legion; and Colonel John, commandant of the Royal Edinburgh Artillery, all retired to Scotland when the wars were over. Anne was wife of Maj.-Gen. Alexander MacLeod, and Frances was wife of Donald Macdonald of Cuidrach, her cousin.

Major Alexander Macdonald of Cuidrach, and his wife, Annabella Macdonald, had the following issue:

I.   KENNETH,* d. Feb. 13, 1814. Aide-de-Camp to Gen. Donald Macdonald at Moore's Creek Bridge. Married a daughter of Nicolson of Scorribreck. The family monument at Forres is inscribed thus:

In memory of Capt. KENNETH MACDONALD
84th Foot Regt. of Caroline Hill, Skye,
and his wife Jane Nicholson.
Also their daughter Jessie, died at Forres,
15th June, 1857.
Mary, long resident in Forres, died in Edinburgh, 11th May, 1898, aged 95.

II. JAMES, married Isabella, daughter of Rev. Donald Macqueen,** Skye, Capt. at Moore's Creek. Prisoner of war for two years in Maryland. Rejoined the King's Army in N.Y. Died of fever 1780.

III. DONALD.*** Ensign Tarlton's Br. Legion 1780. In

---

*   A daughter, Fanny, was wife of John Munro, Forres, Scotland.

**   Brother of Rev. William. Their mother, Florence, was daughter of William Macdonald, styled "the Tutor," uncle of Sir Alexander, of "the 45."

***   Arrived in North Carolina Christmas 1774. Given 500 acres in Anson Co. by his grandfather, Capt. Hugh Macdonald. Returned to London, 1783.

1790 married his cousin Frances, daughter of celebrated Flora. Emigrated to Australia.

IV. FIRST WIFE of James Macdonald, tacksman of Skeabost and merchant in Portree, son of John Macdonald Heisker, North Uist, with issue, among others:

1. EMILY, wife of Capt. James Macdonald of Flodigarry.

   a. JESSIE was wife of Ninian Jeffrey, with issue, among others:

      (1) Agnes Johanna, wife of Ranald Livingstone, with issue:

         (a) Col. Ranald J. (Livingstone-Macdonald, d. 1926).

         (b) Alex.

         (c) Wm. John.

         (d) Emily Nina.

         (e) Mary Frances.

         (f) Flora Charlotte.

V. JANET, wife of her cousin, Major Alexander Macdonald, of Courthill House, Kishorn, Loch Carron, d. Nov. 19, 1815. He was son of Rev. Hugh of Portree, son of Hugh of Glenmore, son of Sir James Macdonald, 2nd Baronet of Sleat. Janet died at Stornoway 1847, buried in Skye. They had issue:

1. ALEXANDER, unmarried.

2. HUGH PETER, of Monkstadt, d. July, 1868, married Jessie, daughter of Donald

Macdonald, Second of Skeabost, with
issue:

a. ALEXANDER, married, with issue.
b. DONALD, married Jessie Macdonald of
Balranald, with issue, among others:
(1) Hugh.
c. HUGH, married Eleanor Crisp with
issue.
d. JESSIE, wife of Mr. Crisp with issue.
e. JULIA, wife of Mr. Crisp with issue.
f. JOHN, married with issue.
g. JAMES, d. 1928, aged 85, unmarried.
(All above went to Australia.)
h. MARGARET, wife of Mr. Todd, with
issue:
(1) Hugh M. Todd, London, married
Margaret, daughter of Inspec-
tor-Gen. Wm. MacLeod, M.D.,
C.B., R.N.
(2) Andrew, Dunedin, N.Z., with
issue, among others:
(a) Bruce.
i. BOSVILLE, wife of Mr. Ross, with issue,
among others:
(1) Sybella, wife of Frank Grey Smith,
solicitor, Melbourne, d. 1926, with
issue:
(a) Ross, solicitor.
(2) Nancy, wife of judge Macindoe.

(3) Sybella.

j.   JOHANNA, unmarried.

k.   ELIZA, unmarried.

3.   ELIZABETH, pursuant to marriage contract
dated at Mugstot, Skye, Oct. 6, 1813, married Alexander MacLeod, of Borlin, Skye
(eldest son of William MacLeod, b. 1750,
d. at Borlin, Skye, 10th Aug., 1811, of
Luskintyre, Harris), without issue. Elizabeth died at Stornoway in 1872, where
she is buried.

4.   ALICE, b. about 1805, d. May 27, 1870, wife
of Roderick Millar, M.D., d. 1889 (son of
John Millar, M.D.), of Stornoway, with
issue:

a.   JOHANNA ELIZA, b. Nov. 10, 1844.

b.   JANETTA MACDONALD, b. Sept. 6, 1846,
both now residing in Edinburgh and
dispensing cheerful Highland hospitality and Highland history.

VI. JACOBINA, b. in Carolina. In 1805 or 1806 she
married Adjutant John (Eon) Macdonald,
Skye, of Lord Macdonald's Regiment. He
is said to have died about a year after their
marriage.

VII. MARION.

20. Marion Macdonald, daughter of Major
Alexander and Annabella, was wife of

Captain Murdoch MacLeod, of Cuidrach, Skye (a branch of the Lewis and Raasa MacLeods), with issue among others:

I.   Alexander, married, with issue, Banna.
II. Marion, wife of Mr. Macintyre, with issue, among others:
     1.   Mary.
     2.   Margaret, wife of Rev. George Rainey Kennedy, minister at Dornoch, in 1868, with issue, among others:
          a.   George Rainey.
          b.   Harry A. A., prof., Edin.
III. Margaret, wife of Rev. Alexander MacLeod, minister of Rogart Free Church, Sutherland-shire, in 1868, without issue.
IV. Malcolm, emigrated to Cape Breton.
V.   Annabella.

21. Annabella MacLeod, daughter of Capt. Murdo MacLeod, by his wife Marion Macdonald, was wife of Dr. James Munro of Kilmuir, Skye. She was born in 1792, and emigrated to P.E.I. in 1841. She died at Alberry Plains, in August, 1852.
22. Marion Munro, daughter of Dr. James Munro, by his wife Annabella, was wife of Peter Nicholson, miller of Orwell.
23. Isabella Nicholson, daughter of Peter

Nicholson by his wife Marion Munro, was wife of John A. Macqueen, farmer, of Orwell.

24. James, Matilda Brown, Malcolm A., and Peter I. Macqueen, are the surviving issue of John A. and Isabella Macqueen.

The MacLeods of Glashvin
(Pinette)

Malcolm MacLeod of Glashvin, Skye, and his wife, Effie Macdonald, of the Glengarry branch of that clan, arrived in Belfast, on the *Polly*, in 1803. The issue of Malcolm and Effie MacLeod were:

I.   Christina, born in Skye about 1782, d. in Orwell, about 1862, wife of Donald Macqueen, with issue.
II. Anne, wife of Alexander MacLeod, Skye, with issue:
1.   John, who married his cousin Christina Macqueen, with issue:
a.   Donald, Orwell, d. May 3, 1885, aged 53, married Catherine, sister of Old Captain MacLeod, with issue, among others:
(1) Murdoch, of Vancouver.
b.   William, of Sentie, Vernon River, who married his cousin Christina MacLeod of Glashvin, with issue, among others:
(1) Margaret, wife of Lemuel Hayden.
(2) Malcolm.
(3) Angus.
(4) Daniel.

(5) Bertha.

(6) Katherine.

III. ANGUS (Big) of Glashvin, d. Jan. 28, 1885, aged 88, married Margaret Dockerty, of Skye, d. Dec. 11, 1863, aged 64, with issue:

1. KATHERINE, wife of Ewen Martin, Eldon, with issue.

2. JOHN, Sentie, Orwell River, d. Jan. 13, 1908, aged 89, married Mary Martin, of Wood Islands, d. July 13, 1888, aged 64, with issue, among others:

   a. JOHN, on the old homestead, married Miss Jenkins, Seal River, with issue:

      (1) Benjamin, married, with issue.

      (2) Margaret, wife of James Murdoch Campbell, Banker, Ceres, California, formerly of Uigg.

3. MARY, wife of Allan Finlayson, Eldon, with issue, among others:

   a. MALCOLM, married Belle Anderson, Orwell Cove, with issue:

      (1) Minna

      (2) Florence, wife of Charles Nelson.

      (3) Alene, wife of Frank S. Reeves, Lot 48, with issue:

         (a) Malcolm.

         (b) Frances.

      (4) William, married Miss Ross, with issue.

          (5) Mary, wife of John James Macdonald, Glashvin, with issue.

4.   Donald A., b. Feb. 26, 1826, d. June 30, 1916, merchant, Eldon, married Ann Mackenzie, Flat River, b. Oct., 1835, d. Mar., 1926, with issue:

    a. Malcolm James, D.D., New York City, married, with issue.

    b. Daevina, wife of Dr. Harry K. Johnston, Charlottetown, with issue.

    c. Hector A., Banker, Hutchinson, Kansas, married, with issue.

    d. Ada, wife of Arthur G. Putnam, Banker, Sackville, N.B. with issue.

5.   Anne, wife of Angus Martin, Eldon, with issue.

6.   Christina, b. 1828, d. 1924, wife of William MacLeod, Sentie, Orwell River, with issue.

7.   Mary, wife of Hector Mackenzie, Flat River, with issue:

    a. Margaret, wife of John Francis Martin, M.D., Eldon, with issue:

        (1) Margaret.
        (2) Elizabeth R.
        (3) Hector David.
        (4) Mary, wife of Blair MacMillan, Calgary, with issue:
            (a) Aubrey, Barrister.

(b) Francis (B.Sc., U. of Alta.).

(c) Angus Malcolm.

(d) Christine.

8. MALCOLM, unmarried.

9. MARGARET, unmarried.

10. ANGUS, Glashvin, Pinette, married Catherine McRae, Point Prim, with issue:

a. CYRUS.

b. MALCOLM, on the old homestead, married Alene Macphee, with issue:

(1) Bell, wife of Rev. Mr. Cleave, Sask., with issue:

(a) John William, 46th Batt., killed in action at Vimy, Flanders.

11. EFFIE, unmarried.

12. SARAH, wife of Robert MacWilliam, Eldon, with issue.

IV. MALCOLM, West River, married Miss MacLean, Point Prim.

V. DONALD, Surrey, married Miss McLeod, with issue.

VI. CATHERINE, wife of Mr. McFayden, West River.

VII. MARY, wife of Findlay Dockerty, Glashvin, with issue in Seal River, and Victoria Cross.

VIII. CATHERINE, wife of Angus Dockerty, with issue, among others:

1. DONALD.

2. MALCOLM, St. Peter's Road, Cardigan.

IX. William, Point Prim, d. Feb. 5, 1885, aged 85, married Mary Lamont, with issue, among others:
1.   Eunice, wife of Roderick MacLeod, Point Prim, with issue, among others:
   a.   Essie.
X.   William, b. Skye, 1783, d. 1850; married Catherine Macpherson. Emigrated to Uigg in 1831. Issue:
1.   Malcolm.
2.   John.
3.   Donald (soldier in Civil War).
4.   Angus.
5.   Alexander.
6.   Norman.
7.   Effie.
8.   Mary.
9.   Katherine.
10. Jessie, wife of Angus R. MacSwain, Lorne Valley, with issue:
   a.   Christie A., wife of H. E. Gurney.
   b.   Daniel.
   c.   Mary.
   d.   William and two others.

Murdoch "Tailor" MacLeod
and Family of Orwell Crossroads

Murdoch MacLeod was born in Harris, Scotland. At an early age he joined the navy and fought in the Napeolonic Wars, being present at the Battle of Trafalgar, according to family tradition on the Victory. He emigrated to P. E. Island in 1816, and after living in Flat River a number of years he married Mary MacLeod, a cousin of Neil MacLeod, who lived near Orwell Bridge. Prior to 1840 he took up a hundred acre farm, and on it built a log cabin a few yards west of Orwell cross-roads. This farm was later increased by additions on the east and west sides, until there were about four hundred acres occupied by himself and his three sons, Alexander, Murdoch and Neil. Murdo's descendants occupy these farms today.

To distinguish this family from the numerous other MacLeods in the district they were always known as "Tailor." Murdoch Tailor died at Orwell, May 23, 1860, aged 76. Both himself and consort are buried in Belfast churchyard. Their issue were:

I.   RACHEL, wife of William MacLeod, Lyndale, with issue: six daughters and one son, Donald, at present living on the old homestead in Lyndale.

II. MARGARET, wife of Norman MacSwain,

Portage, Belfast, without issue.

III. DONALD, in U.S.A.

IV. JOHN, married Miss Nicholson, Orwell Cove, without issue.

V. WILLIAM, Dundee, married Catherine Biggs, Newtown, with issue, among others:

    1.   NEIL, Orwell, married Elizabeth Musick, Kinross, with issue:

         a.   PERCY.

         b.   EVELYN, wife of Otis MacLeod, of Uigg.

    2.   MURDOCH A., b. 1864, d. Nov. 1927, married Jessie Munro, Alberry Plains, with issue:

         a.   ALICE, wife of Mr. Stewart.

         b.   GWENDOLINE, wife of John Mackay.

         c.   MUNRO.

         d.   GLADYS, wife of Ernest Charlton.

         e.   MARGARET, wife of Mr. Campbell.

         f.   MARY.

         g.   IVAN.

         h.   ARTHUR.

VI. BELLA, d. 1927, aged about 93, wife of Allan Buchanan, Mount Buchanan, with issue.

VII. NEIL, d. Aug. 25, 1910, aged 81, married Isabella McDonald, d. March 13, 1892, sister of Peter Findlay MacDonald of Orwell, with issue, among others:

    1.   NEIL.

2.   MURDO.
3.   MARY.
4.   CHRISTY.
5.   BELLA.
6.   JESSIE, on the homestead.

VIII. CATHERINE, d. 1903, wife of Donald MacLeod, Orwell, with issue, among others:
1.   MURDOCH, Vancouver.

IX. MURDOCH, b. Nov. 8, 1832, d. Sept. 17, 1917, married Anne H. Enman, d. May 12, 1893, aged 44, daughter of David Enman, Vernon River, with issue, among others:
1.   LAWRENCE, living on the old homestead.
2.   FRANK.
3.   FLORENCE.
4.   MARY, wife of William Greenwood.

X.   NORMAN, d. July 5, 1889, aged 63, Dundee, married Margaret Buchanan, with issue.

XI. ANNE, b. Jan. 8, 1842, wife of Richard Wood, Orwell, with issue, among others:
1.   CYRUS.
2.   NORMAN, married Miss Macpherson, Dundee, with issue.
3.   MARY JANE, wife of Mr. McInnis, with issue.

It is believed that Mrs. Wood is the only woman living whose father was a combatant in the Battle of Trafalgar. At 87 years of age she is in excellent health.

XII. Alexander Sr., b. in Orwell, one of the ablest and most astute business men P.E.I. ever produced. Master Mariner, and ship owner; this masterful character was recognized as one of the most sagacious and capable seamen of his day. He owned the farm adjoining the one on which his father lived, and when his business career was over settled down to a life of useful retirement. He died on June 14, 1893, aged 70. His devoted wife, Jessie Campbell, who was born in Skye, died on January 18, 1893, aged 70.

Captain MacLeod was part owner of, and for many years commanded, the S.S. *Gulnare*, employed by the British Government in surveying and charting the coasts of Eastern Canada and Newfoundland. So wide a reputation had he as mariner that, when the first Atlantic cable was being laid, he was employed as advisor in connection with the work on the Newfoundland coast. On his retirement from command of the *Gulnare* he was succeeded in command by his son Alexander, Jr.

To Alexander MacLeod, Sr., and his wife Jessie Campbell, were born the following children:

1. Murdoch, living in Texas.
2. Archibald, B.A., M.D. (McGill), d. Oct. 15, 1884, aged 25 years; one of the first to

practice medicine in New Westminster, B.C.

3. NORMAN, b. 1852, Vancouver, married Mary Ann MacSwain, daughter of Alexander MacSwain, of Portage, Belfast, d. Nov., 1927, aged 77, with issue:

   a. FLORETTA, wife of Professor Lemuel Robertson (M.A., McGill), Vancouver, with issue:

      (1) Norman (B.A., U. of B.C., Oxon.) Rhodes Scholar, married Henriette J. Welling, The Hague.

      (2) Mary (U. of B.C.), wife of John C. Oliver.

      (3) Barbara (U. of B.C.).

   b. MAXWELL, Nanaimo, married Henrietta McLaren, with issue:

      (1) Maxwell McLaren.

   c. MARY, wife of George Beveridge, with issue:

      (1) James.

   d. SAMUEL A., married, without issue.

4. HUGH D., b. 1856, d. April. 15, 1927, married, first, Katherine A. Munn, of Orwell, d. Sept. 22, 1893, aged 37, with issue:

   a. JESSIE, wife of Oscar Nielson, Vancouver, with issue, one daughter.

   b. MAY, wife of Alexander Stevens, Vancouver, son of Dowager, Lady Peel, England.

Hugh married second Jessie Munn, with issue:

c.   MILDRED.

d.   ADA.

5.   ALEXANDER, JR., Master Mariner, b. 1858, d. April 26, 1909, married Kate, daughter of Alexander Mackinnon, Orwell North, with issue surviving:

a.   DANIEL ALEXANDER.

b.   JESSIE, wife of Malcolm Buchanan with issue:

(1) Anne, wife of John MacLeod, with issue:

(a) Leslie, married, with issue.

(b) Helen.

6.   JOHN O., Vancouver, married Anne Mutlow, Orwell, with issue:

a.   WILLIAM, married, with issue:

(1) Jessie, wife of Frank Donaghy, with issue.

Donald Ban Oig MacLeod
of Murray Harbour Road

Donald Ban Oig MacLeod, of Valtos, Skye, emigrated to Prince Edward Island with the Uigg
colonists in 1829. His wife Mary Martin, was sister
of John Martin of Stenscholl, Skye, the father of
Samuel Martin, of Uigg. Their issue were:

I. Donald, b. 1818, d. 1896. Taught school on
    P.E.I. for a few years, and after visiting Scot-
    land returned to Canada. At Linwick, Que.,
    he married Mary Noble. He moved to Nairn,
    Ont., and after spending a few years there,
    settled in Parkhill, Middlesex Co., where he
    died. Their issue were:
    1. Emma, wife of William Thompson, of
        Windsor, Ont., with issue:
        a. Stewart Thompson, killed in action
            overseas.
    2. Martha, wife of Peter Stewart, Calgary,
        with issue:
        a. Neil, Dunblane, Sask.
        b. Gordon, Calgary.
        c. Stanley, killed in action overseas.
    3. David Noble, Edmonton, married Jean
        Waters, with issue:
        a. Douglas (C.E., U. of T.), killed in
            action overseas.
        b. George (C.E., U. of T.).

       c.   Helen, wife of Gordon Crozier, banker, Walkerton, Ont.

       d.   Agnes (B.A., U. of Alberta), Edmonton.

    4.   Mary Priscilla, wife of Colin MacNiven, Marshall, Minnesota, with issue:

       a.   Mary.

    5.   Matilda, Winnipeg.

    6.   Frederick, Los Angeles, married Anna Kinnisten, with issue:

       a.   Donald Keith (E.E., McGill).

    7.   Edward Alexander, Parkhill, married Clara Holt, with issue:

       a.   Murray.

    8.   Katalena, Minneapolis, U.S.A.

II.   John, married with issue.

III.   Malcolm, d. in Nebraska, married, first, Anne McPhee, d. 1866, of Brown's Creek, P.E.I., with issue:

    1.   Malcolm, b. Dec., 1844, married, with issue.

    2.   Jessie, b. April, 1847, wife of Mr. Wight, Quincy, Mass., with issue.

    3.   Donald, b. Sept., 1849, married, with issue.

    4.   John J., Uigg, b. 1851, married Mary Finlayson of Leith, Scot., with issue:

       a.   Louise.

       b.   Malcolm.

    5.   Rev. Donald Ban, b. Aug., 1854, d. May,

1918, married Elizabeth Dyer, with issue:

a. ELIZABETH, wife of Rev. William C. Wauchope (Harvard), Buford, Georgia.

Donald Ban married 2nd Mary J. MacLeod, Kinross.

6. CHARLES, b. Aug., 1856, married, with issue.

7. ANGUS CHARLES, b. Aug., 1859, Langley, Wash., married, with issue.

8. RODERICK, b. Jan., 1861, married, with issue.

9. HUGH, b. May 13, 1863, Attorney-at-Law, Langley, Wash.

10. MURDOCH WILLIAM, b. April 22, 1866, Langley, Wash., married, with issue.

IV. RODERICK, b. 1822, in Skye, d. 1896, at Murray Harbor Road, married Marjory, daughter of his first cousin, Charles Martin, of Heatherdale, P.E.I., with issue, among others:

1. FLORA, b. 1848, now of Grandview, widow of Alexander Gillis, with issue:

a. JOHN ALEXANDER, Murray Harbor Road.

b. RODERICK.

c. CHARLES.

d. MARJORY.

e. MINNIE.

f. ALEXANDER.

g. SADIE.

h. ELIZABETH.

2. Marjorie, wife of Malcolm Gillis, Lyndale.
3. Charles.
4. Christy, wife of Capt. Neil Campbell, Oakland, Cal., with issue:
   a. Wife of Capt. William Mayne.
5. Donald C., broker, State of Washington, b. 1859.
6. Malcolm.
7. Mary, wife of Mr. Livingston.

V. Samuel, Murray River, married, with issue.
VI. Nancy, married with issue.
VII. Margaret, wife of Mr. Livingstone, High Bank, with issue.
VIII. Catherine, wife of Malcolm Martin, Brown's Creek, with issue, among others:
   1. Charles, Belmont, Manitoba, married, with issue, among others:
      a. Emily.
      b. May.
      c. Ellen, of Winnipeg.
   2. Samuel, Belmont, Man., married, with issue, among others:
      a. Catherine, wife of Dr. Stevenson, Belmont.
   3. John, Los Angeles, California.
   4. Daniel, Los Angeles, Cal., married, with issue.

The MacQueens of Orwell

Donald Macqueen, of Skye, and his wife Christina MacLeod, daughter of Malcolm MacLeod of Skye (later of Glashvin, Pinette), emigrated on the *Polly.** After living for a few years near Macaulay's Wharf, Glashvin, Pinette, Donald Macqueen died, and was buried in the French cemetery, Belfast, P.E.I.

About 1815, the brave mother, with her six helpless children, moved to Orwell and took up a hundred acre farm on the north bank of the river. This was later divided between her two sons, Angus, who took the half fronting on the river, and John, who took the north half. Widow Macqueen died about 1864, aged over eighty, and was buried in the Belfast cemetery.

They had the following children:

I. CHRISTINA, b. in Skye, about 1802, wife of her cousin, John MacLeod, with issue, among others:
    1. WILLIAM (SENGIE).
    2. DONALD.
II. MALCOLM, b. February 18, 1804, d. Oct. 29, 1886, married on Feb. 2, 1830, Margaret

---

*   Among other members of the family two brothers, John and Angus, remained in Skye.

Martin, of Newtown, b. 1806, d. Nov. 5, 1892, with issue:

1. DONALD, b. March 5, 1832, d. 1915, unmarried.
2. SARAH CATHERINE, b. Sept. 8, 1834, d. Sept., 1895, wife of William Ferguson, miller, Cardigan, d. 1907, with issue, among others:
    a. PETER, married Minnie Macaulay, with issue.
    b. MARION ADELLE, wife of Kimpton McGrath, Lorne Valley.
    c. WILLIAM HENRY.
    d. MARGARET MAY.
    e. ELSIE CATHERINE, wife of Munro McGrath, Lorne Valley.
    f. JOHN THOMAS.
    g. ROBERT ELLIOT.
    h. MINNIE FLORENCE.
    i. WINNIFRED MATILDA.
3. JOHN ANGUS, b. March 10, 1836, d. May 25, 1918. On May 5, 1871, married Isabella Nicholson, b. 1845, d. July 3, 1926, with issue surviving:
    a. JAMES, b. July 3, 1873.
    b. MATILDA BROWN, b. Mar. 17, 1877, wife of Walter D. Ross, Kinross, with issue.
    c. MALCOLM ALEXANDER, b. Dec. 8, 1878, married Harriet Murgatroyd Riley, Winnipeg.

d. PETER ISAAC, b. Dec. 15, 1880, married Bella Irene Ross, Kinross.

e. MARGARET ALICE.

f. MARION MUNRO.

g. CYRUS.

h. GEORGE FRANKLIN.

i. CHRISTINA.

j. JOHN ANGUS, all died in youth unmarried.

4. CHRISTINA, b. July 17, 1839, d. June 16, 1913, wife of Malcolm Dockerty, Cardigan, d. Oct. 4, 1896, with issue:

a. KATE, unmarried.

b. ROBERT, married Adelaide Birt, Mount Stewart, with issue:

(1) Malcolm Birt, b. Sept. 19, 1909.

(2) Stuart Mills, b. Feb. 20, 1911.

(3) Cyrus Alexander, b. Nov. 4, 1914.

c. MARGARET, wife of Jonathan E. Birt, Mount Stewart, with issue:

(1) Barbara.

(2) Gladys.

(3) Ida.

(4) Chester.

d. ANNE, wife of James McEachern, Cardigan, with issue:

(1) Christina.

(2) Florence.

e. OLIVER, married Laura Vionette, Lunenburg, N.S.

      f.   Jean, wife of George Jardine, with issue:

          (1) George S.

5.   Peter Alexander, b. March 26, 1842, now living in Townsville, Australia, married Elizabeth Parnham Marshall Neilsen, daughter of James Neilsen, with issue:

      a.   Peter Angus, married Ethel Cruckshank, with issue, among others:

          (1) Cedric.

          (2) Dulcie.

          (3) Elizabeth.

      b.   Jessie Marshall.

      c.   Isabella Burt, wife of Mr. Cruckshank, Townsville, with issue:

          (1) Reginald.

          (2) Nancy.

          (3) Leslie.

          (4) Ronald.

      d.   Malcolm Towers, Aus. Exp. Forces, died in Australia of wounds received in action, Flanders.

      e.   Leila.

      f.   Orwell, Aus. Exp. Forces, killed in action in Flanders.

      g.   Adelaide.

6.   Alexander Robert, b. Nov. 26, 1845, d. May, 1910, New Glasgow, married Nellie Williams, Cardigan, with issue:

a. GEORGINA GERTRUDE, wife of John Goodwill Macphail, C.E., Ottawa, with issue:
(1) Andrew.
(2) Catherine.
b. HERBERT, married Anne Barbara Logan.

III. JOHN, b. 1806, d. Nov. 5, 1879, Orwell North, married, March 10, 1836, Katherine MacLean, Montague River, b. 1819, in Uig, Skye, d. 1915, with issue:
1. DONALD, d. April 1, 1886, aged 46, married Anne Shaw, Uigg, with issue:
a. KATHERINE.
b. JOHN D., Uigg.
c. MARGARET, married Mr. Grant with issue.
2. WILLIAM, Butte, Montana, unmarried.
3. ALEXANDER, married Elizabeth Steele, St. John, N.B., with issue:
a. ARTHUR.
b. WILLIAM.
c. GRACE.
d. JANET.
4. MALCOLM, b. 1844, d. 1912, married Sarah MacKinnon, with issue, Hamilton, N.Y.; and married second Katherine Nicholson, Orwell Cove, with issue:
a. WILLARD.

    b. Louise.
  5. Mary, b. 1853, d. 1917, unmarried.
  6. John, b. 1856, d. 1901, unmarried.
  7. Hugh, b. 1858, d. 1912, unmarried.
  8. Margaret, b. 1846, unmarried.
  9. Christine, unmarried.

IV. Flora, b. 1808, wife of Donald Lamont, Lorne Valley, with issue, among others:

  1. Christy, wife of John Johnson, Lorne Valley, with issue:

    a. George.

V. Angus, Orwell, d. June 6, 1876, aged 67, married, Margaret (Kinloch) Macdonald, d. April 10, 1903, aged 88, with issue:

  1. John, Victoria Cross, married Lois Mellish, with issue:

    a. Frederick.

    b. Angus.

    c. Laura.

  2. Daniel, married Miss Hay, St. John, N.B., with issue:

    a. Verna.

  3. Alexander, Calgary, unmarried.

  4. Daniel, Jr., d. 1927, unmarried.

  5. Margaret, wife of Mr. Fraser, San Franscisco, without issue.

  6. William.

  7. Angus, b. 1853, d. Jan. 7, 1911, Orwell, unmarried.

8. MARY, wife of Neil MacNeill, Wood
    Islands, with issue:

    a. ANGUS.

    b. ALBERTA, married, with issue.

    c. CASSIE, wife of James A. Campbell,
        C.E., Oakland, Cal., with issue:

        (1) Roderick.
        (2) Malcolm.
        (3) Daniel.
        (4) Margaret.
        (5) William.
        (6) Minnie.

VI. CATHERINE, d. Mar. 31, 1871, aged 57, wife of
     Donald Shaw, Uigg, d. Jan., 1883, son of Allan
     Shaw, Flat River, with issue:

     1. DONALD A., d. July 12, 1874, aged 32, mar-
         ried Miss Masters, Vernon River, with
         issue:

         a. CATHERINE, wife of Angus Martin,
             Glen Martin.

     2. ANNE, d. 1915, wife of Donald Macqueen,
         Uigg, with issue.

     3. KATHERINE, wife of D. Shaw, High Bank.

     4. CHRISTY, wife of Mr. MacLean, Dundas.

     5. ALLAN, Uigg, d. Feb. 3, 1915, aged 74, mar-
         ried Flora Shaw, High Bank, d. April 12,
         1906, aged 52, with issue surviving:

         a. JOHN ERNEST, Uigg, married Murdina
             MacLeod, Newtown, with issue:

      (1) John Allan.

      (2) Catherine.

    b.   FLORENCE, wife of George Johnstone, Lorne Valley.

Malcolm Macqueen [II above] was one of the first children born in Belfast. After living with his widowed mother on the river farm until about 1833, he leased, and afterwards purchased from Louisa Augusta, Lady Wood, wife of Sir Gabriel Wood, and Maria Matilda Fanning, daughters of Governor Fanning, the homestead fronting on Fletcher's road, a short distance east of Orwell cross-roads. To this new farm he moved, across the frozen Nicholson marsh, the frame dwelling house, which was used until 1859, when a nine-room house was built. This was the home of the family until in 1895 it was replaced by the one now in use.

Of average height, he was a man of powerful physique. In an age when books were possessed by the few, memory was cultivated to a degree that is not thought necessary today. In this respect he was a marked man. There was stored in unusual measure in his retentive memory the folklore of the distant Highlands, as well as a complete knowledge of his native Belfast. He was as true a Highland Seannachie as if he had been born and lived in Skye.

His wife, Margaret Martin, of Newtown, was a woman of delicate body, and refined intelligent mind. Fortunately refinement of mind and manner is not confined to those living in luxurious surroundings. Mrs. Albert Jenkins recently spoke of her and others of her neighbors, who were born in an age when wants were few, as possessing innate refinement and gentility of manner to a degree equalling, if not surpassing, that aimed at in modern ladies' schools.

Their son, John Angus, was born on the old homestead on which he died, near Orwell crossroads. He was even more characteristically Highland than his father. In a community where honesty was as common a quality as chastity, he was distinguished for it to a degree that made business relations with him a thing of mathematical exactitude. He was outspoken and uncompromisingly honest. No act inconsistent with the strictest integrity was ever imputed to him. In all his relations with his fellow men he was distinguished by a virtue, defined as "punctuality." Four generations came and went and he was still in the same place. He is reported never, in that time, to have missed a Sunday in church, and never to have been late for service. The regularity of his life made him an unchanging and continuing institution in the district.

If there was any announcement to be made

in church that was omitted from the minister's agenda, he would calmly arise in his pew, and facing the audience amend the omission in an unembarrassed tone. He knew the Bible from cover to cover, and was satisfied with nothing less than a Scriptural sermon. One day he became impatient at the wanderings of a clergyman into politics, and is reported to have rebuked him, almost in the words of Queen Elizabeth, who "when the Dean of Saint Paul's, at a public sermon, enunciated some observation that displeased her, threw open the window of her private closet, in which she always worshipped, and shouted to him 'leave that ungodly digression and return to your text.'"

To him character was the one and only test of worth and position. He recognized no other ground for social distinction.

Possessing the variable Highland temperament, he would pass from brooding melancholy to Highland gaiety with electric speed. The changing moods of the elements awoke in him a ready response, and he watched the varying phases of wind and sky, foretelling with mystifying accuracy what the elements had in store. In an age of superstition, living among people who inherited and believed in it, he was practical to an unusual degree, and scorned what he could not demonstrate from actual experience.

Order was a passion with him, and the child who failed to return to its designated place any instrument or tool, was the recipient of a well earned rebuke. Deceit and dissimulation were entirely foreign to his nature. No one was ever left in doubt as to his estimate of him. It seemed perfectly natural and proper to disclose frankly his likes and dislikes. One possessed of so many virtues is usually austere and uncompromising by nature. For their virtues such men are respected, to a certain extent feared, and to a less extent loved. His physical strength was great almost to the end. In all his long life he was never treated by a physician. At seventy-eight his striking pale blue eyes could detect an open rowboat at Point Prim seven miles from where he stood.

His wife, Isabella Nicholson, had an insatiable appetite for the things of the mind. With the ardor for education that characterises the Scottish people, she engaged in the daily tasks, not infrequently with an open book or newspaper clipping beside her, to be perused at every favorable opportunity. Her knowledge of history, and of the involved inter-relations of families, not only in her native province, but among the great in foreign lands, was so intimate that she was known among her friends as the "historian." The death of five of her children after reaching maturity failed to crush her indomitable will; each recurring blow of fortune seemed to strengthen her power to meet the one to follow. With her own temper in complete subjection, she was wont to rebuke the ill tempered and passionate in the words, "greater is he that controlleth his temper than he that taketh a city."

THE MARTINS OF UIGG
AND MURRAY HARBOUR ROAD

John Martin, Stenscholl, Skye, and his wife Catherine Macdonald of Snizort, Skye, arrived in Uigg in 1829. Their family consisted of:

I. HUGH (B.A. Glas., 1849-51, M.D. New Orleans), surgeon in Confederate Army in Virginia, married Ella McCarthy, Virginia, with issue:
    1. REV. HUGH MACDONALD MARTIN, Baltimore.
    2. Two daughters.
II. CATHERINE, wife of Murdoch Nicholson, Head Montague, with issue.
III. MALCOLM, married Catherine, daughter of John (Small) Macdonald, Belfast, with issue.
IV. DONALD, Orwell Head, married Miss Macdonald, Grandview, with issue:
    1. MARGARET.
    2. HUGH.
    3. MARJORY, wife of Alex. Ross.
    4. DUNCAN.
    5. JOHN.
    6. JOHN DONALD.
    7. ANNE.
V. CHARLES, unmarried.
VI. JOHN, died in Virginia, about 1869, unmarried.
VII. SAMUEL, b. in Skye, Sept. 25, 1821, d. in Uigg,

married Sarah, daughter of James Campbell, of Uigg, b. Point Prim, 1829, with issue:

1. MARGARET, b. 1850, d. 1871, wife of John Martin, Kilmuir, P.E.I., with issue, one daughter.
2. HUGH, b. 1853, d. 1923, Sheboygan, Wisconsin, married Emma Balzer, with issue, five children. One son served overseas in A.E.F.
3. JOHN SAMUEL, Uigg, Speaker Local Legislature, P.E.I., born 1855, married Hattie Mackenzie, with issue surviving:
    a. EMILY.
    b. ANNE.
    c. SAMUEL.
    d. JAMES.
    e. HUGH, living on the homestead with his parents.
    f. JOHN, b. July, 1896, 105th Batt. C.E.F., d. May 22, 1919, from wounds received in action.
4. CHRISTY ANN, b. 1857, wife of George Wood, Milwaukee, with issue, four children.
5. CATHERINE, wife of Kenneth MacLean, Alberry Plains, with issue, eight children.
6. JAMES CAMPBELL, minister, b. 1861, married Miss Livock, Chaplain overseas with C.E.F.

7. MARJORY, wife of Lauchlin McKay, Dundas, with issue: nine children, of whom William, Hugh, and George served overseas with the C.E.F. The latter was killed in action in Flanders.

8. EMILY, wife of Fred Beers, Mass., with issue: six children, one son served overseas in A.E.F.

9. SARAH, wife of John G. Mackenzie, Granville, P.E.I., with issue: nine children, one of whom, George, was killed in action overseas with C.E.F.

10. JOHN DONALD, Orwell, b. 1868, d. 1922, married Ella Mackenzie, with issue, five children.

11. MALCOLM CAMPBELL, minister, California, Chaplain with A.E.F., b. April 1, 1871, married Ella May Parks, Minneapolis, with issue:
    a. JUNE.
    b. MARGARET.
    c. ELEANOR.

12. SAMUEL ANGUS, minister, Manitoba, Chaplain overseas with C.E.F., b. Sept. 3, 1873, married Nettie Fielding, with issue surviving:
    a. JEAN, wife of Ernest Yeo.
    b. WALLACE JAMES.
    c. MARGARET.

Samuel Martin [VII above] and his wife, Sarah Campbell, were a very unusual and distinguished couple. They were parents of fifteen children, of whom thirteen reached maturity. Four were school teachers, and three were successful clergymen. Two served overseas as chaplains in the Great War. In the same war eight grandsons of Mr. and Mrs. Martin were engaged. Three of them were killed in action.

In every good and worthy cause Mr. and Mrs. Martin and children were always found in the forefront.

The Martins of Newton, Belfast

The first member of this family to arrive on Prince Edward Island was Donald Martin, who was born at Snizort, Skye, in 1759. His wife, Marion MacLeod of Applecross, was born in 1770. She was sister of Rev. Kenneth MacLeod, and cousin of the famous Rev. Dr. Norman MacLeod. They arrived in Belfast on the *Polly* in 1803, with their family. After living for a few years in Point Prim, they moved to the Newtown River, where, by Indenture dated October 13, 1819, Donald Martin leased from Lord Selkirk the homestead which has been occupied by the family continuously from then up to the present time. Mrs. Martin died in 1845, to be followed in 1848 by her husband.

Their issue were:

I. MARY, wife of Mr. Kelly, Cow Bay, Cape Breton, with issue, among others:
    1. MARGARET ELLEN, wife of Mr. Morrison.
    2. CHARLES.
II. KATHERINE, wife of Robert Grant, with issue, among others:
    1. ABIJAH.
    2. DONALD.
    3. PETER.
    4. JOHN.

    5.   Martha, wife of Capt. James Richards, Murray Harbor.

    6.   Mary, wife of John Compton, Belle River.

III. Kenneth, married Alice Moore, with issue:

    1.   Mary, wife of Mr. Lane.

    2.   Sarah, wife of Mr. Moore.

    3.   James.

    4.   John.

    5.   Angus, married Mary Anne Hamilton.

    6.   Daniel, Montague Bridge, married Martha Atkinson.

IV. Margaret, b. 1806, d. Nov. 5, 1892, wife of Malcolm Macqueen, Orwell, with issue.

V.   Peter, b. Nov., 1809, d. April 8, 1877, married Sarah Mackinnon, March 6, 1844, b. Belfast, Sept. 8, 1821, d. Oct. 1, 1914, with issue:

    1.   Sarah Elizabeth, wife of William Mackenzie, Wood Islands, with issue:

        a.   Anne, wife of Horatio Nelson.

        b.   Mary Janet, wife of William McLaren.

        c.   Charles Angus, married to Annie Florence Montgomery.

        d.   William Alexander (M.D. McGill) married Ella, daughter of Luke Kelly, Fredericton.

        e.   Sarah Peter, wife of Charles Hope Beattie, Boston, with issue:

           (1) Janet.

           (2) Ruth.

(3) Sarah.

(4) Margaret.

(5) Mary Louise, wife of John Martin.

(6) Peter Kenneth.

(6) Maud Elizabeth.

2. Kenneth John, K.C., Stipendiary Magistrate, Charlottetown, married Elizabeth Montgomery, with issue surviving:

a. Kenneth.

b. Jean.

3. Donald Charles, K.C., ex-M.P.P.

4. Jessie.

5. Catherine.

6. Charles William.

7. Margaret Ellen, died unmarried.

8. Simon, married.

9. Mary Alice.

10. John.

11. Hannah Louise. These last three live on the old homestead.

VI. John, b. 1811, d. 1862, married Emily Compton, with issue:

1. Mary, wife of William Compton.

2. Peter, married May Smith, Newtown, living in Boston, aged 83, with issue.

3. Daniel, married Sarah Godson.

4. William K.

5. Alexander, married Sarah Anne MacLeod.

6. Sarah, wife of Mr. Bagnell.

7.   Margaret Emily, wife of Mr. Betts.
8.   Louisa Jane, wife of Mr. MacDougall.
9.   Kenneth, unmarried.
10. James Ebenezer.

Portree, 28 June, 1803.

This do certify that the bearer hereof, Donald Martin, a married man, and his wife Marion MacLeod, have to the best of our knowledge during their residence in our parishes, the greatest part of their lives, conducted themselves in a proper, just, decent, honest and industrious manner.

They are poor and have a weakly family of children, and we think them worthy of being received and encouraged in any Christian Society in which Providence may assign their lot. Given, place and date as above, by

(Sgd.) Alex. Campbell, Minister of Portree.

(Sgd.) Mal. McLeod, Minister of Snizort.

Donald Nicholson of Orwell

Among the several families of Nicholsons who arrived on the *Polly* was that of John Nicholson of Stenscholl, Skye, and his wife Jane Martin.

In 1806 John Nicholson and his son Donald, in consideration of the sum of £50 of lawful money of P. E. Island, received from the Earl of Selkirk a grant of five hundred acres of freehold land, of which one hundred and thirty-four acres were on the south side of the Portree Creek or Newtown River, and three hundred and sixty-six acres to the north of said river, and fronting on Orwell Bay. This land was probably occupied in 1803, for in the conveyance dated 1806 it is described as "beginning near the dwelling some time ago and now occupied by the said John and Donald Nicholson along Samuel Martin's land, etc." On his second visit to Prince Edward Island, Lord Selkirk was guest in this house, which stood near the shore, and commanded a pleasing view of Orwell Bay, and the beautiful wooded country extending to the north. Samuel Martin, cousin of Jane, had received his grant for the two hundred and fifty acres adjoining on the north in 1805. Both John and Jane Nicholson were buried in the French cemetery. They had issue:

I.   HANNAH, married in Skye, died on P.E.I. without issue.

II. Rachel, unmarried.
III. Donald, miller, Orwell, Magistrate, b. about
     1780, married Isabella Nicholson, Skye. She
     died about 1855 or 1856, over 80 years of age.
     Both are buried in Belfast churchyard. Their
     issue were:
     1. Hannah, d. May 17, 1881, aged about
         75, wife of William Harris, b. Bideford,
         Devon, England, d. March 12, 1884, aged
         80, at Milton, P.E.I., with issue:
         a. Janet, d. Dec. 17, 1904, aged 68, wife
             of Thomas Darke, Bideford, Devon,
             England, d. at Milton, P.E.I., June 20,
             1884, aged 59, with issue:
             (1) Hannah Jane, wife of Robert Bag-
                  nall, Hunter River, P.E.I., without
                  issue.
             (2) Francis Nicholson, b. Oct. 26,
                  1863, Regina, Sask. ex-M.P., mar-
                  ried Anne Elizabeth Mackinnon,
                  of Milton, P.E.I., with issue
                  surviving:
                  (a) Vernon Frank.
                  (b) Clarence Thomas (U. of T.,
                      Harvard).
                  (c) Trevyln Victor.
             (3) Charlotte Margaret, wife of Ben-
                  jamin Moore, Charlottetown,
                  Royalty, with issue.

    (4) Ellizabeth Lavinia, wife of James P. Moore, Milton with issue.

    (5) Adeline Charlotte, wife of Bruce Mackinnon, Regina, with issue.

    (6) Amanda Janet, wife of Pope Balderson, North Wiltshire, with issue.

2.   FLORA, b. June 27, 1808, d. April 13, 1895, wife of Donald Ross, Uigg, with issue.

3.   PETER, miller, Orwell, b. 1809, d. May 10, 1884, married Marion Munro, daughter of Dr. James Munro, Kilmuir, Skye, b. 1812, d. June 1897, with issue:

a. ISABELLA, b. 1845, d. July 3, 1926, married, May, 1871, John Angus Macqueen of Orwell, with issue.

b. ELIZA, b. 1850, d. 1923, wife of Capt. Alexander William MacLeod, Orwell Cove, d. June 1, 1919, with issue surviving:

    (1) William, married Alma Taylor, with issue, two daughters.

    (2) Marion, wife of Roger Cronsberry, Ottawa, Ont., with issue.

    (3) Mary, wife of George Mutch, Earnscliffe, P.E.I., with issue.

    (4) Benjamin.

Eliza married 2nd to Harold B. Collins.

c. ANNABELLA, b. 1852, wife of Daniel

Nicholson, Victoria, B.C., with issue surviving:

(1) Sadie.

(2) Arthur Stirling, Los Angeles, married Myrtle Singer, with issue:

    (a) Gordon Daniel.

(3) Ruth, wife of Arthur A. Dods, Victoria, B.C., with issue:

    (a) Gordon Arthur.

4. MARY, died in youth.

5. MARGARET, wife of Donald Macphee, Miller, Heatherdale, with issue, among others:

    a. REV. SAMUEL D. MACPHEE (Dal., Pine Hill), b. Feb. 10, 1865, d. Oct. 26, 1913, married with issue:

        (1) Margaret, wife of her cousin, James Nicholson, Orwell Cove, with issue.

6. ISABELLA, wife of John Donald Matheson, born Skye, emigrated to Uigg, 1829, d. March 3, 1876, aged 74, with issue, among others:

    a. RODERICK, married with issue.

7. JANE, Earnscliffe, b. March 20, 1814, d. March 28, 1899, unmarried.

8. JOHN, died in youth.

9. CHRISTINA, d. June 20, 1885, aged 60, wife of Alexander MacLeod, Earnscliffe, d. Oct. 3, 1893, aged 73, with issue, among others:

    a.   RACHEL LAVINIA, wife of Mr. Walker, Westboro, Mass., with issue:

       (1) Annie.

       (2) Joseph.

    b.   CHARLOTTE EUNICE, wife of Mr. Ward, Mass.

    c.   MALCOLM J., b. June 27, 1860, married Sarah Dockerty, Seal River, with issue:

       (1) Gordon.

       (2) Sydney.

       (3) David Sutherland (B.A., Dal., Pine Hill).

       (4) Eva.

IV. JOHN, Orwell Cove, d. Nov. 10, 1866, aged 74, married Mary MacLeod, Orwell Cove, d. 1886, aged 87, with issue, among others:

    1.   DONALD, married Miss MacMillan, Wood Islands, with issue, among others:

       a.   JAMES, on the old homestead, married Margaret Macphee, with issue, six sons and four daughters.

In 1804 or 1805 Donald Nicholson [III above], who later operated the mill on Orwell River, returned to Skye. On the voyage a heavy storm was encountered. It was thought all would be lost. After the tempest abated he composed a Gaelic poem, which, during the early history of Belfast, was on everyone's lips. Today in the Orwell district a few persons only are able to repeat it, among them being Mrs. Malcolm MacLeod and Margaret MacLeod (Peggy Neil). In this poem the author recounts the violence of the storm, and the danger to ship and passengers. That women only have preserved the poem may be due to its stirring appeal to their more romantic nature. The author pictures himself on his way back to his beloved Skye to meet his intended bride, who, spinning and knitting, waits anxiously for her fond sweetheart, then in the extremities of a peril so dire that he may never return to her.

In 1805 or 1806 he returned to Prince Edward Island with his bride, on the *Rambler*, bringing several new immigrants from Skye and adjoining parts, who settled in Flat River and Belle River districts.

He was shipping agent for Lord Selkirk, and in this capacity made frequent trips to Halifax and other parts in connection with the lumber industry.

In the early days of the settlement news was preserved in form of poetry. When the first log house, in which the family lived, was consumed by fire the event was commemorated in a Gaelic ballad which recounts, among other incidents, that the bed curtains went up in smoke. Two other log houses succeeded this one in succession. In one of them lived Rachel, and to this day the field about is known as Rachel's field.

The Rosses
of Kinross, Uigg and Eldon

Lauchlin Ross, and his wife Catherine Martin, emigrated from Strath, Skye, in 1821. They and several friends and relatives occupied the whole territory between Orwell Bridge and Murray Harbor Road in that year. On July 15, 1848, Mr. Ross died aged 78. Their issue were:

I. Donald, b. July 27, 1804, d. Dec. 9, 1856, married Flora Nicholson, b. June 27, 1808, d. April 13, 1895, with issue:

    1. JOHN, b. Feb. 25, 1835, d. Dec., 1908, Hamilton, Ontario, married Rachel Rogers, Lampton Mills, Ontario, with issue:

        a. FREDERICK HENRY.

        b. EDWARD D.

        c. LUCIEN GREY.

        d. VIVIAN.

        e. RAYMOND REGINALD.

    2. DAVID, Kinross, b. Dec. 12, 1837, d. March 15, 1913, married Mary Louise Enman, b. 1854, d. May 28, 1915, with issue:

        a. MARY ELIZABETH, wife of Murdoch Peter Macdonald, Orwell, with issue.

        b. JOHN FREDERICK, married Mattie Huntley, with issue.

        c. JANETTE FLORENCE, married, with issue.

        d. ARTEMAS ENMAN, married, with issue.

    e. Donald.

    f.   Bella Irene, wife of Peter I. Macqueen.

  3. Margaret, wife of James Hayden, with issue.

  4. Janetta, wife of Lemuel Hayden, with issue:

    a. Sidney.

    b. May.

    c. Charlotte.

  5. Lauchlin.

  6. Donald.

  7. Alexander, married Marjory Martin, with issue.

  8. Christy Hannah.

  9. Mary, unmarried.

  10. Annabella, unmarried.

II. David, d. Feb. 10, 1890, aged 80, married Anne Martin, Belle River, d. Feb. 22, 1899, aged 79, with issue:

  1. Alexander.

  2. Daniel C., K.C., Toronto, died Sept. 5, 1929.

  3. Katherine, wife of Daniel W. MacLeod, Sentie, Vernon River, with issue:

    a. Dr. William.

  4. Christy, wife of Jeremiah Smith, Newtown, with issue.

III. Alexander R.

IV. Isabel, wife of John MacLeod, Kinross, with issue:

1. ALEXANDER, married with issue:
   a. JOHN WALTER.
   b. ANGUS A.
   c. BELLA.
V. WALTER, Eldon, d. March 29, 1875, aged 55, married Catherine Murchison, Point Prim, d. April 9, 1915, aged 83, with issue:
   1. MARGARET.
   2. DANIEL.
   3. MARY ALICE.
   4. CHARLOTTE.
   5. FLORENCE.
   6. CATHERINE.
   7. BELLA.
   8. LAUCHLIN.
   9. SAMUEL.
   10. DAVID.
VI. KATHERINE, wife of Murdoch Macdonald, County Line, with issue.
VII. DONALD, JR., d. Sept. 11, 1892, aged 68, married Isabel Macdonald, Belle River, d. Nov., 1920, aged 86, with issue:
   1. ANGUS ALEXANDER, Lieut. Royal Artillery, d. 1900, Malta, married, with issue.
   2. LAUCHLIN, d. 1920, unmarried.
   3. ALEXANDER (M.D., Trinity), d. 1926, married Mary Campbell, with issue:
      a. FLORENCE, wife of Mr. Neameyer, with issue:

(1) Lulu, wife of Mr. Arkinstall, with issue:

(a) Myrtle, wife of Mr. MacLeod, with issue:

(i) Kenneth.

(ii) Malcolm (B.A., M.D., McGill).

(iii) Hector (U. of B.C.).

4. Katherine, wife of Benson Weatherbee, with issue.

5. Christy, wife of James MacLeod, with issue:

a. J. Milton.

b. Alice, wife of Preston McIntyre (B.A., M.D., McGill).

c. Beulah.

d. Blanche.

e. Lucretia.

6. Isabella, wife of Ansley Goodwin, Pugwash, N.S..

7. Walter Donald, Kinross (Dal.) married, Matilda Brown Macqueen, with issue:

a. David Douglas, b. March 24, 1913.

b. Marion Isabel, b. Sept. 9, 1916.

Rev. Samuel MacLeod

Norman MacLeod, one of the 1829 settlers, died in Uigg in 1837, aged 75. His wife was Margaret, daughter of Donald Macphee of Skye. His parents were, Neil MacLeod and his wife Sophia Nicholson.

Mr. and Mrs. MacLeod were accompanied to P.E.I. by their children, Samuel, Roderick, John, Murdoch, Mrs. Angus Macdonald, Mrs. James Macdonald, Mrs. Cameron and Neil, who lived in Vernon River.

I. Samuel taught school in Pinette and Flat River. There he married Margaret Currie, who had emigrated to that district with her family from Mull, Scotland. From 1840 to 1870 he was minister of the Baptist Churches in Uigg and Belfast. He died on August 23, 1881, aged 85. His wife died on February 27, 1902, aged 95. Their children were:

1. Norman, d. July 1928, aged 91, married, with issue:

    a. Hammond.

    b. Samuel.

    c. George R. (McGill), Asst. City Engineer. Montreal, married Margaret Furness, with issue.

    d. James D. (B.A., Acadia), minister, married, with issue.

2. MALCOLM, d. April 29, 1903, aged 64, married Esther Robertson, East Point, d. Sept. 12, 1923, aged 73, with issue:

    a. SAMUEL, on the old homestead, married Miss Vaniderstine, with issue, among others:

       (1) Florence.

    b. ELLA.

    c. ALEXANDER R. (B.A., McGill), Rhodes scholar, barrister-at-law, Vancouver, married, with issue.

    d. MARGARET.

    e. DUNCAN, married with issue.

    f. HADDON SPURGEON (Guelph Agr. Col.).

3. JAMES (M.D., McGill), Charlottetown, married Margaret Alma Gates, d. 1927, with issue, among others:

    a. DR. MACLEOD, Moosejaw.

4. DUNCAN (B.A., McGill), barrister-at-law, Charlottetown, unmarried.

5. SARAH, wife of William MacLeod, Bridgetown, Dundas, with issue.

6. MARY, unmarried.

II. RODERICK, d. June, 1888, aged 85. His wife Catherine, d. Dec. 2, 1882, aged 75. Among their issue were:

1. MALCOLM, K.C., for two generations the leader of the bar, and the outstanding man on the Island.

2. John, unmarried.
3. Ann, d. March 4, 1905, aged 58, wife of Alexander Martin, M.P., Valleyfield, b. March 14, 1842, d. April 13, 1921, with issue:
    a. Albert J. (Dal., Cornell), C.E., Montague.
    b. Belle, wife of H. W. H. Knott, barrister, Montreal.
4. Katherine, died 1929, unmarried.

III. John, married Rachel, daughter of Donald Gordon. She died January 11, 1915, aged almost 98. Without issue.

IV. (Big) Murdoch was born in Skye in 1815, and died July 29, 1889. On October 6, 1837, he married Margaret Gunn in Miramichi, N.B. She died August 26, 1916, aged one hundred all but two or three months. They had several children. Of these John Murdoch, one of the most successful farmers on P.E.I., lives on the old homestead. He was born April 20, 1848. He married his cousin, a daughter of "Little" Roderick MacLeod of Uigg Rear, sister of the late judge Neil MacLeod, of Summerside. Their son and only child, Otis, with his wife Evelyn MacLeod and children, live with them. Another son of Big Murdoch is William MacLeod, a well-known resident of Bridgetown, Dundas, P.E.I.

Other Belfast Families

James Macdonald, d. Sept. 12, 1883, aged 90. His son Donald, married Margaret, daughter of Donald Gordon. Their son, Donald Gordon Macdonald, of Vancouver, the well-known Baptist minister, was 86 in February, 1929. His brother, Capt. Malcolm, of Georgetown, was father of Mrs. Richardson, wife of the late H. A. Richardson, General Manager of the Bank of Nova Scotia.

The MacHamish MacLeods who at one time lived on Farm 10, now part of John MacLeod's farm, were notable for their great size. Their average height was about six feet two inches. James was six feet five, Roderick six feet four, Alexander six feet two, Christy, Mary and another sister were all about six feet. They moved to the U.S.A. in the eighties.

Alexander MacLean, miller, Montague River, who came from Skye in 1829, died December 10, 1878, aged 80. His wife Margaret Macdonald d. April 13, 1899, aged 68. Their daughter Catherine, wife of John Macqueen, died when about 96.

On the triangular parcel of land near the Baptist Church lived Alexander Nicholson. One of his sons was Rev. Alexander B. Nicholson (b. 1845) for many years professor of Classics at Queen's University, Kingston. Another son, John, was a banker, in Ellis, Kansas.

In Orwell lives MRS. SAMUEL JARDINE, daughter of the faithful Frederick Augustus Kidson,* for many years minister of the Baptist churches at Uigg and Belfast, died South Maitland, N.S., July 3, 1912, aged 83. Edith, one of her seven daughters, lives with her.

NORMAN MURDOCH MACLEOD of Uigg, later of Orwell River, and his wife, who was Miss MacLean of Portage, Belfast, moved to Charlottetown where in partnership with J. D. MacLeod he carried on an extensive grocery business. His daughter Mary (d. Sept. 1929), after graduating in music in Paris, France, married Dr. Macdonald, Calgary. Marion is wife of Dr. G. F. Dewar, Charlottetown, Maud is widow of Dr. Stuart Carruthers, Catherine lives in Charlottetown. Murdoch, Sidney and Milton live in Alberta.

PETER GORDON of Uigg, brother of Rachel and Margaret Gordon, was father of J. A. Gordon, M.A., D.D. (b. June 24, 1844), the distinguished and eloquent Baptist minister, now of Montreal, who was the centennial orator at Uigg, 1929. The latter is father of: Alva H. Gordon, one of the leading physicians of Montreal; Peter W. of Hamilton; Herbert of Ottawa; and John P., who, with Samuel MacLeod, owns the well known dry goods firm.

---

* Frederick Augustus Kidson is the son of Samuel Augustus Kidson of Hereford, England.

Moore and MacLeod, Charlottetown.

The said Samuel MacLeod is great-grandson of
Alexander MacLeod (Allistair Taillear), who, with
his family including Murdoch, emigrated from
Raasay, Scotland, in 1821, where they had gone
a few years earlier from Skye. They bought the
four-hundred-acre farm extending easterly from
Orwell bridge along the Kinross road, paying
therefor £195 currency. Descendants still own
half of this farm. Donald, son of Murdoch, and
father of Samuel, built a stone house on it and to
this day the family is known as Stonehouse.

Murdo Raasay, as he was generally known,
was a remarkable man. Before leaving Scotland
he married a Miss Martin, a connection of the
Orwell Cove Martins. Her brother Samuel was
one of the first teachers in Orwell. Murdo used
to spend much time on the commanding height
beside the Kinross road on his estate. Here with
artist's eye, he loved to scan the panorama spread
before him. Looking westerly there was unfolded
to his view a scene of matchless charm and beauty.
At his feet the Orwell river gently hurrying on its
ever widening way to join the distant sea. On the
left the wooded hill, with here and there a clearing
flecked with daisies, fell gently from imposing
height to the water's edge beneath. On his right
heavily timbered low lands, patched with settlers'
clearances, stretched far away northward.

The little mound still visible on the hill-top marks the final resting place of one who would not be parted from the place he loved so well even in death.

www.ingramcontent.com/pod-product-compliance
Lightning Source LLC
Chambersburg PA
CBHW051713020426

42333CB00014B/963

* 9 7 8 1 9 2 6 4 9 4 2 7 2 *